Prism

a theological forum for the United Church of Christ

Volume 22, Number 2, Winter 2007

PRISM: A Theological Forum for the United Church of Christ is sponsored by the seminaries of the United Church of Christ. As a journal for the whole church, its goal is to offer serious theological reflection from a diversity of viewpoints on issues of faith, mission, and ministry. Views expressed in PRISM are those of the authors and do not necessarily reflect those held by the editorial board of the sponsoring seminaries. PRISM Publishers, Inc., a Minnesota corporation, is independent of the United Church of Christ and United Church Press.

PRISM is published twice a year. Subscriptions are $12.00 for one year (two issues) and $20.00 for two years (four issues). Add $5.00 for addresses outside the United States of America. Payment must accompany order and be made in United States dollars. Some back issues are available for $6.00 per copy. Subscription orders and changes of address should be sent to United Church Press, 700 Prospect Avenue, Cleveland, OH 44115-1100.

Editorial correspondence may be sent to either of the co-editors:
Lee Barrett, Elizabeth Nordbeck, Andover Newton Theological School, Newton Centre, MA 02459 (617-964-1100).

ISSN 0887-5049

Volume 22, Number 2, Winter 2007

CONTENTS

EDITORIAL

It is a daunting prospect to take up the responsibilities of Clyde Steckle as he retires from being co-editor of *Prism,* a journal that he helped found twenty-two years ago. For eighteen of those years Clyde's thorough familiarity with the United Church of Christ, his participation in its life in multiple contexts, his theological acuity, and his sensitivity to social and cultural developments enabled him to discharge his editorial responsibilities with rare judiciousness. I can only hope that the mentoring of co-editor Elizabeth Nordbeck will enable me to reflect a little of Clyde's commitment to the lively and serious theological conversation in the United Church of Christ that is *Prism's* purpose.

This is the second of two issues celebrating the 50th anniversary of the United Church of Christ. In this issue we look at our half-century heritage from a variety of perspectives, considering ecclesiology, theology, social ethics, new congregations, and a variety of other topics. These essays are not motivated by antiquarianism or nostalgia, but by a desire to understand the path that we have traveled together so far in order to discern the present contours of our church and its possible future trajectories.

Elizabeth Nordbeck's "Unfinished Business" explores the seeming paradox that the denomination is self-consciously rooted in two thousand years of Christian history but nevertheless intentionally remains a "work in progress." She identifies several areas in which this dialectical tension has generated challenges for the UCC, including the need to theologically nurture members both new and old (many of whom have entered the UCC from other traditions) across a broad theological spectrum, the need to clarify and nuance what we mean by "inclusivity" in such a way that it neither degenerates into unrestrained relativism nor sanctions a return to a restrictive orthopraxis, the need to explore the relationship of autonomy and accountability in such a way that accountability is given its due, and the need to retrieve our ecumenical audaciousness. Throughout the essay Nordbeck celebrates the UCC's avoidance of ultimate temporal certainty or completeness as a spiritually appropriate response to the sovereignty of God and the limitations of human creatureliness.

Richard Taylor's and Marjorie Royle's "The New United Church of Christ" considers the intentional new church starts, the adopted congregations (from other traditions), and the "pop-ups" (newly formed congregations that subsequently affiliate with the UCC) that have joined the UCC since 1957. These congregations are significant for our common life because 10% of all members of the UCC are members of congregations that did not exist in 1957. Because many of these congregations are not composed of persons of European ancestry, they significantly contribute to the multi-ethnic and multi-cultural character of the UCC. Because many of them were birthed in regions with a previously low UCC population, such as Florida, they also contribute to the geographic diversity of the UCC.

Donald Freeman's article examines the fifty years of social and ethical teachings expressed in General Synod statements and actions. The statements of the General Synod were selected as indicators of the ethical perspectives informing the history of the UCC because they are the denomination's nearest approximation to a church-wide voice. Freeman shows how some types of issues have waxed and waned in our brief history. The predecessor denominations' focus on labor issues, industrialization, and urbanization was augmented in the 60's by concerns for race relations, international relations (including the Vietnam war), arms control, and human rights. In the 1970's and 80's the economic disparities spawned by globalization, threats to the integrity of the environment, the empowerment of women, and the rights of sexual minorities became foregrounded. Freeman notes that some concerns, such as economic marginalization and the need for peace with justice, have remained relatively constant. Throughout this history another permanent feature is evident: the denomination has appealed to all four sides of the "Wesleyan quadrilateral" (Scripture, tradition, reason, and experience) to guide its ethical reflection.

Lee Barrett's essay investigates a tension that parallels Nordbeck's paradoxes: the tension between theological identity and theological diversity. Barrett argues that the UCC has always exhibited profound theological diversity, and that the roots of this diversity are not always traceable to differences among the predecessor denominations. Rather, the most serious and deep-rooted theological divergences in the UCC have been produced by the tensions between four different sets of visceral existential anxieties and four different hoped-for resolutions. In other words, different theological parties in the UCC have been animated by four different basic hopes and fears, and have lived in four different "theological worlds." Three of these worlds have been prevalent in the denomination from 1957 to the present, and were found in each of the ancestor traditions. None of these theological worlds show any signs of disappearing, a fact that accentuates the need for a mutually enriching conversation across theological lines.

In a different way, Theodore Trost's article also explores the issue of denominational identity through the investigation of the history of the "God Is Still Speaking" campaign. Trost considers the campaign in terms of the tension between "identity," the unifying convictions and values of a community, and "identification," the way a community presents itself to outsiders. Trost notes that the denomination's strategies for public identification to outsiders may sometimes have been in tension with many of the insiders' sense of identity. Most significantly, Trost shows how an appeal to personal experience may have functioned as the primary locus of authority in the campaign's conception and development.

While devoting less attention to the history of the UCC, the other essays also explore the relationship of new eccesial possibilities to older commitments within the denomination. Bruce Epperly employs the model of "mind/body" interaction to envision healthier ways for congregations and judicatories to relate to seminaries, and vice versa, in order to imagine a more vital future for the church and its ministries. The essay by William Imes exhorts the church to embrace multiple styles and paths of preparation for ministry (as mandated by the General Synod of 2005) in order to honor the particularities of local contexts and traditions.

One way or another, all of these essays unearth a series of dialectical tensions energizing the first fifty years of the United Church of Christ. Each of these tensions has something to do with the countervailing pressures of the desire for latitude and openness on the one hand, and the longing for a coherent sense of identity and historical continuity on the other. Most of the articles find value in both poles of the tension, and celebrate the UCC's willingness to live with the sometimes exhilarating and sometimes disquieting uncertainty. Perhaps the humble admission that on this earth finite and sinful creatures such as ourselves cannot aspire to a permanent resolution of these tensions will create in us a space in which the Holy Spirit can more freely move.

We invite your comments, critiques, and suggestions, and your manuscripts about matters of theological concern in and to the United Church of Christ. Please feel free to contact any of us by e-mail: Beth Nordbeck (enordbeck@ants.edu); Lee Barrett (lbarrett@lancasterseminary.edu); Jack Lynes (jwlynes@aol.com).

– Lee Barrett

UNFINISHED BUSINESS

What is the "Still-Speaking God" Saying to the United Church of Christ at Fifty?

Elizabeth Nordbeck

[Portions of this article were presented at the 2007 meetings of the Vermont and Central Atlantic Conferences]

"The unfinished church." This was the way writer and editor Jean Caffey Lyles described the United Church of Christ in an article published in *Christian Century* during the early 1980s. I no longer remember the exact context—perhaps Lyles was writing around the time of the denomination's 25th anniversary, when the UCC was beginning its first formal round of self-examination—but the idea of an "unfinished church" seems unusually prescient. As a way of understanding aspects of our denominational distinctiveness, the description is as appropriate today as it was a quarter century ago. To be sure, in an eschatological sense **all** expressions of the Church, from ancient Roman Catholicism to the adolescent UCC, are "unfinished." Only God knows when (or how, or if) Christ will return and call true believers to himself in a final and complete church triumphant. But arguably the United Church of Christ is "unfinished" in certain distinctive—more important, in certain **deliberate and governing**—ways that reveal its half-century-old commitment to change as a hallmark of faithfulness.

This apparent intentionality is both intriguing and revealing. In 1957, when the denomination was formed, no one had yet heard of a "God is Still Speaking" campaign, with its implicit suggestion that God's guiding words to us are not frozen in third century language and cultures. No one had noted publicly that Christians should be careful not to place periods

Elizabeth Nordbeck serves as Moses Brown Professor of Ecclesiastical History at Andover Newton Theological School and is a co-editor of Prism.

where God places commas because the faithful Christian life is often more about journey than destination. Where, then, did this defining "ethic of incompleteness" that Lyles observed come from? Perhaps one source is the familiar admonition of Pastor John Robinson who, tradition claims, told his departing flock of Pilgrims that "God has yet more light and truth to break forth from his holy word." Or perhaps it was inspired by New England poet James Russell Lowell, who on the eve of the Mexican-American and the Civil Wars wrote these familiar lines, later included in the popular hymn, "Once to Every Man and Nation:"

> New occasions teach new duties
>
> Time makes ancient good uncouth
>
> We must upward still, and onward
>
> Who would keep abreast of truth.[1]

Whatever the source of their convictions, architects of the fledgling UCC took pains to build into their new denomination a concrete understanding that "keeping abreast of truth" and faithfulness to God demand living in the midst of paradox. On the one hand, faithful living requires trust in a reliable God who is "the same yesterday, today, and tomorrow." On the other hand, faithful living demands trust in that same **surprising** God who continues to discomfit and challenge us by "making all things new." Life (including, especially, the life and practice of the church) therefore demands a kind of holy tentativenesss, an expectation that in God's great scheme of creation things of this world are, indeed, unfinished and will surely change. Alone among today's Protestant denominations, the United Church of Christ seems to have built that paradox into its self-understanding and—more remarkably—into its foundational commitments and structures.

Consider this. The *Basis of Union*, a document that preceded and guided the planned merger of the Congregational Christian Churches and the Evangelical and Reformed Church, went through multiple changes and ten drafts between 1942 and 1948. One section of the document that remained constant, however, was the affirmation that "denominations exist not for themselves but as parts of that Church, within which each denomination is to live and labor, and, if need be, die." This was followed by an expression of hope "that in time soon to come, by further union between this Church and other bodies, there shall arise a more inclusive United Church."[2] In other words, the denomination's founders both hoped and expected that the church they were intent on establishing would, from the beginning, understand itself as unfinished; that someday, God willing, it might intentionally go out of business, becoming a different entity altogether.

Or consider this. Roger Shinn, now professor emeritus at Union Theological Seminary in New York City and the major drafter of the denominational *Statement of Faith* adopted in 1959, has commented that the *Statement* was "written to be re-written." Certainly this is something few would dare say about, for example, the Apostles' or Nicene Creed, or the Westminster Confession! And in fact, the UCC's *Statement* **has** been re-written, not once but twice: first in 1977 and again in 1981, primarily to express changing views about theological language and gender. [3]

How is it that after such a short time the United Church of Christ can so easily alter an historic consensual statement, like the *Statement of Faith*, that expresses the beliefs once "commonly held among us?" Consider this. The *UCC Constitution*, adopted in 1960 and declared in force a year later, has been amended a dozen times; the appended *Bylaws* have been amended more than twenty times. But one constant has been the second paragraph of the Preamble. Here, in six brief theological affirmations, architects of the United Church of Christ grounded the new denomination firmly in orthodox Protestantism. Yet among these short statements are two remarkable sentences:

> [The United Church of Christ] claims as its own the faith of the historic Church expressed in the ancient creeds and reclaimed in the basic insights of the Protestant Reformers. It affirms the responsibility of the Church *in each generation* (italics mine) to make this faith its own in reality of worship, in honesty of thought and experience, and in purity of heart before God.[4]

The United Church of Christ, in other words, understands itself to be firmly rooted in two thousand years of Christian history and tradition. Nevertheless, the UCC also understands itself to be a permanent "work in progress"—not, presumably, because the press of culture demands it, but because a still-speaking God commands it.

In God's great plan for the ages—and in much of human history— fifty years is a very short time, often with few observable changes. Historically, moreover, significant change in the churches has occurred even less rapidly than in the surrounding culture. But this last half-century has been different. No doubt some readers of this article were not even alive in 1957. (In that year, I was ten years old, dimly aware that something significant was happening to the Congregational churches of my parents and great-grandparents.) When the United Church of Christ was born, Fidel Castro had not yet become premier of Cuba. John Kennedy was neither president nor slain hero, and most Americans did not know what a "fundamentalist" was. America was recovering briefly between two different wars -- in the throes of a cold war with the now-defunct Soviet Union, and on the brink of internal strife over civil rights. Automobiles had huge tailfins to make them resemble the rockets that Americans and Soviets were racing to launch into space; no one gave a thought to "fuel economy." No one had yet heard of personal computers, cell phones, FAX machines or ipods; no one knew about suburban sprawl, test tube babies, Wal-Mart, or inclusive language. Church attendance had spiked to record highs in the mainline denominations (although this phenomenon was short-lived), and Pentecostalism was perceived—if it was perceived at all—as a fringe movement among the economically disenfranchised.

This was the world into which a new, unfinished United Church of Christ was born, boldly declaring its infant self ready to change and, if necessary, to die. Today, a little more than half a decade into the 21st century, every American is familiar with the vast changes—technological, social, ecological, scientific, political, demographic—that have occurred during the last fifty years. The rapidity and depth of those changes have almost certainly been greater than at any other equivalent time in human history. But what about the United Church of Christ? At the half-century mark, has the "unfinished church" lived up to its initial commitment to be faithfully responsive "in each generation"? And where is it going as it marches toward a centennial anniversary?

Without doubt, there have been changes. Cultural pluralism, globalism, gender orientation, homophobia, immigration, sexism and women's rights, accessibility, Christian unity, interfaith dialogue, ecological awareness: these are a few of the emerging issues that have affected the denomination's public theology, its social agenda, and its internal structures and policies. The past fifty years have seen a move from New York to Cleveland, better to represent the diversity of origin and emerging constituencies in the church; an ecumenical partnership with the Christian Church (Disciples of Christ)—perhaps the most fully developed relationship, short of organic merger, among American Protestant denominations; one major and several lesser restructures; the publication of *Book of Worship* and two hymnbooks, including a still-controversial *New Century Hymnal* that has encouraged theological conversation and raised questions about theological orthodoxy; and a *Manual on Ministry* that has morphed from a thin pamphlet to a four-inch-wide ring-bound notebook. Clearly (and, no doubt, as the founders planned it) this is not our grandparents' United Church of Christ. In the next few paragraphs, then, I want to focus on several areas in which our unfinished denomination has changed and may be called to change further if it is to remain faithful during its next fifty years..

The first of these unfinished areas is membership. In 1957 the new United Church of Christ was comprised of more than two million members, in roughly 8,000 churches. About three-quarters of these were members of the Evangelical and Reformed Church, and 1.3 million were members of the Congregational Christian Churches. Although there are no statistics to prove it, it is likely that a high percentage were birthright believers, lifetime members of one of the four founding denominations. In 1957 the United Church of Christ was a national body with its greatest numerical strength in those regions where immigrants and founders from the constituting traditions had settled or eventually moved: New England, Pennsylvania, the old Northwest territories, parts of the lower Midwest, California. There were few churches in the southeast and relatively few in the far northwest and southwest.

Today's United Church of Christ has a somewhat different profile. Membership totals roughly 1.2 million—a significant loss, though not unique among mainline Protestant denominations. Roughly 6,000 congregations remain; nearly 800 of these were planted after 1957. Many churches have membership of under 100 persons. The denomination is still regional, but the regions have expanded; Florida and California, for example, claim the largest number of new congregations. (For a complete demographic assessment see "The New United Church of Christ," by Richard H. Taylor and Marjorie H. Royle, elsewhere in this issue of *Prism.)* There are still no statistics regarding members' churches of origin, but my own "soft" data suggest that in many if not most churches well under fifty percent of congregants typically claim birthright membership in either the UCC or one of its four founding bodies.[5]

Today, when people in the UCC think about membership, they often think about a revival of evangelism and new growth. For example, in 2002, the Council for Theological Education of the United Church of Christ asked several reflectors to describe their vision of the denomination in the year 2020.[6] "We want to know what you think God is doing with and through the United Church of Christ," the directions specified. Not surprisingly, the responses focused on creative outreach to new constituencies. One writer imagined a "fantasy" United Church, growing in numbers and vitality in part because of its ability to help people handle complex realities in a changing world. Another writer described the church of the future as "unlikely," that is, as a growing, countercultural church whose leadership, membership, worship, and theological convictions will be unlike those of any other churches. Still another focused on the now-familiar calling of the UCC to grow into a church that is multicultural, multiracial, open and affirming, and accessible to all. Interestingly, however, no one mentioned the "new members" who are already here. To what might a still-speaking God be calling us with respect to our membership?

That the UCC needs to re-think and re-vitalize evangelism is surely true. **But I believe God may, first of all, be calling this unfinished church to do some things differently with the women and men we already know, the**

ones who have found their way into our local churches. Who are they? They are former Baptists and United Methodists, Unitarian-Universalists, and Pentecostals. They are former Roman Catholics and Evangelical Covenanters. They are from the right and left ends of the theological spectrum, as well as from the middle. They are people who have sojourned in many religious groups—and in none—before joining a local United Church of Christ congregation. Here, too, the data is soft. But arguably the United Church of Christ is attracting people from across a very broad theological spectrum. No doubt this is, in part at least, because of the minimalist nature of our formal theological convictions—those six foundational statements mentioned above. Here is what the Preamble states:

> The United Church of Christ acknowledges as its sole Head, Jesus Christ, Son of God and Savior. It acknowledges as kindred in Christ all who share in this confession. It looks to the Word of God in the Scriptures, and to the presence and power of the Holy Spirit, to prosper its creative and redemptive work in the world. It claims as its own the faith of the historic Church expressed in the ancient creeds and reclaimed in the basic insights of the Protestant Reformers. It affirms the responsibility of the Church in each generation to make this faith its own in reality of worship, in honesty of thought and expression, and in purity of heart before God. In accordance with the teaching of our Lord and the practice prevailing among evangelical Christians, it recognizes two sacraments: Baptism and the Lord's Supper or Holy Communion. [7]

Our collective willingness to "accept as kindred in Christ" all those who share the confession that Christ is Son of God and Savior means that the United Church of Christ casts a wide and permeable theological net; our collective **unwillingness** to use these or any other doctrinal statements as formal gate-keeping devices does the same. One result of this openness is what I have come to call "accidental ecumenism,"[8] that is, the presence among us of people with vastly different faith traditions, practices, convictions, and spiritual needs. Our congregations are full of men and women who have been nurtured as Christians in other traditions—**and** our congregations are full of spiritually hungry people who have limited experience of any defining Christian nurture or spiritual formation. Both these groups are changing us, often without our conscious awareness.[9] But we have given precious little thought to how *we* are changing **them**, or to how (and whether) we are helping them mature in the faith. Perhaps God is calling us to feed these hungry souls: not just to welcome them—that is easy enough—but also to give them direction, some UCC Christian basics. And if God **IS** calling us to serve these men and women who are already in our pews, what does this mean? Surely at the very least it means no one-size-fits-all membership classes that introduce our Boards of Deacons and active committees, but fail to ascertain whether Christian education of a more foundational sort is needed. Surely, too, it means that pastors and knowledgeable lay leaders need to be able to articulate exactly what "those things commonly held among us" in the United Church of Christ might be—perhaps minimally, the six statements from the Preamble printed above.[10]

The second unfinished area I want to discuss is inclusivity. Central to the UCC at its founding was the understanding that God's realm is an inclusive, not an exclusive one. For some time now, I have been fond of saying that, when it comes to deciding who is in and who is out of Christian fellowship, there are two kinds of people. First, there are those who would rather close the denominational gates quickly to make sure no goats get into the pen with the sheep, lest the herd be irreparably tainted. And then there are those who would rather leave the gate open, because they are so sure it's better to let a few disruptive goats in than to leave any precious sheep out. Clearly, the United Church of Christ is and has been for fifty years among the latter.

In the beginning, our inclusivity was largely related to the melding of four founding traditions that had some things, but by no means all, in common. Early on, church leaders tried to **include** representatives of these traditions when they searched for staff members, when they wrote theological position papers, when they sought to blend liturgical styles and practices. But over time, "inclusivity" grew much, much more inclusive. In the 1970s we became collectively aware of "inclusive language" related to gender—and then, to age, ability, geography and more. With new waves of immigrants arriving in the United States at about the same time, we reached out to "underrepresented constituencies": not only African Americans, who had long been an important presence in both the Congregational and Christian traditions, but also to Hispanics, Asian Americans, and others. In 1993, the denomination declared its commitment to become a more multi-racial, multi-cultural church. Ongoing concern about justice for all God's people led to early affirmation of gays and lesbians as full partners in Christ's Church, and then to bisexual and transgendered persons, as well.[11] "Whoever you are, wherever you are on life's journey, you're welcome in the United Church of Christ." Perhaps the expansion of our understanding of inclusivity came to full fruition in the denomination's recent identity campaign, with its familiar televised images of bouncers expelling "inappropriate" people from **other**, less inclusive churches. To what, then, might a still-speaking God be calling us with respect to our understanding of inclusivity?

I believe God may be calling this unfinished church to clarify and nuance its understanding of inclusivity. No other word in the contemporary UCC lexicon has had more pervasive and controlling force among us—nor so little public reflection on its theological and practical meaning. By comparison, we may look at the word "covenant," which also has enjoyed great force and currency in shaping UCC identity and behavior. "Covenant," of course, is a word with a long past, with roots in ancient Mesopotamia and the Bible as well as in the writings of the Protestant Reformers. But it has also been thoughtfully and thoroughly considered, in the fifty years since 1957, as a controlling theological idea for the United Church of Christ. Louis Gunnemann, Reuben Sheares, Donald Freeman and Bill Hulteen—and I myself—have all published essays and articles about covenant and its meaning in and for the United Church of Christ.

But not so "inclusivity." This is a word UCC members use routinely—both in local congregations and, especially, in wider church settings. But what does it actually signify, with respect to our behavior and our self-understanding? "Whoever you are, wherever you are on life's journey, you are welcome here." Do we—**should we**—mean that, without exception? Let me offer two brief stories to illustrate the dilemma I perceive.

The first story was told to me by a former student. The choir in her church was open to all who wished to sing, and one evening a young woman, who had been present for a number of Sunday services, came to rehearsal. She candidly admitted that she was actually a member of the Unification Church—more familiarly, a "Moonie"—but as a self-identified Christian and musician she was eager to have a good choir with which to sing regularly. Soon it became apparent that she was not only interested in singing, but in energetically talking about her own faith tradition. Eventually, when enough people complained, she was asked to leave.

Here is the second story. Some years ago, I was asked to be a weekend "theologian in residence" at a large, urban United Church of Christ congregation. My tasks were to teach several classes and workshops and to preach. Soon after I got there, I was cautioned to ignore a particular individual if he raised his hand or sought to question me during one of these sessions. He was, I was told, a once-brilliant man who had allegedly "burnt out" experimenting with drugs during the 1960s. Unwilling to bar him altogether from the church, where he was a regular attendee at both worship and educational events, members of the congregation had developed a formal policy of ignoring him, lest his rambling questions and comments be disruptive.

Whoever you are, wherever you are in life's journey, you're welcome here? Evidently there **are** some limits—and perhaps you will agree with me that there should be some, for the sake of the good order of our churches.[12] But what basic principles govern this notion of inclusivity and define its boundaries? There is, within the United Church of Christ, widespread (and, I believe, admirable) agreement that "welcome" is about our churches' being open and affirming, multi-cultural and multi-racial, and accessible. But this is only a shallow and partial understanding of welcome; there is much more to be discussed. For example, how should a newcomer (or an old-timer) be "welcomed" when he or she is consistently obnoxious and disruptive? Are there ever times when one's behavior becomes so egregiously problematic that welcome may legitimately be compromised or withdrawn? Or again, are members and attendees welcome to hold theological opinions that are radically different from those commonly held in the United Church of Christ, even if they intentionally use a congregation's theological openness to undermine its historic identity and commitments? Make no mistake: I am convinced that our attempt to offer "radical hospitality" is the **right** way to go about following Jesus. But even Jesus' own welcome to all was not unconditional; surely he pondered deeply those moments when his acceptance and forgiveness were dependent upon another's "going, and sinning no more." If inclusivity is to remain a controlling—and compelling—metaphor for the United Church of Christ, it is time we explored fully what it means.

The third unfinished area I want to mention is the changing relationship of autonomy and accountability—and particularly our emergent understanding of the nature of accountability. I do not need to remind readers of *Prism* that in 1957 those of Congregational heritage did not go gently into this good merger. For many of the latter group—and although I was ten years old at the time, I must count myself among Congregationalists—it was "hell, no, we won't go!" unless there were formal guarantees of the absolute, inviolable autonomy of the local church. After years of wrangling, even lawsuits, Congregationalists got the assurance they wanted, now codified in the current *Constitution and Bylaws* in exactly the same words as in the original 1960 iteration: "The autonomy of the local church is inherent and modifiable only by its own actions."[13] Article Five, Paragraph eighteen goes on to detail all the things a local church can do, unimpeded by any external authority: everything from hiring ministers to owning and selling property. Even so, some remained nervous. Here, for example, is an excerpt from records of the Hopkinton, New Hampshire, Congregational Church, which did not vote to join the United Church of Christ until 1969:

> Moved that the First Congregational Church of Hopkinton shall become a member of the United Church of Christ *Provided,* however, that this action does not confer upon the United Church of Christ or any of its officials or representatives any authority to imply or infer that it has a right to express an opinion in our behalf on any subject of a controversial nature, be it religious, social, economic, or political, unless this church has specifically so authorized; and further *provided* that if in any manner or at any time any present right or privilege of this Church shall be limited or affected by any action of the General Synod of the United Church of Christ or any of its subordinate organizations,

> or by any amendment to the Constitution or By-Laws of the United Church or any of its subordinate organizations, then this Church shall have the right to withdraw from the United Church at any time thereafter, and the Church shall not forfeit this reserved right by any delay, however prolonged.

In the years since 1957, some things have changed. In New England, especially, churchfolks still jealously guard their autonomy. But increasingly, throughout the churches, UCC members are comfortable pairing **autonomy** with the idea of **accountability**, by which is generally meant a mutual sense of obligation, even sacred obligation, one to another. It was church historian Louis Gunnemann who in the 1970s first used the word "covenant" to describe associational relationships within the United Church of Christ. This usage was developed later by Reuben Sheares, head of the former Office for Church Life and Leadership. Sheares argued that United Church polity is best described as covenantal: each setting of the church listens to, honors (without necessarily supporting) and strives to cooperate with, each other setting.

In the most recent iteration of the *Constitution and Bylaws,* a new Article 3, entitled "Covenantal Relationships," was added to make these intra-church relationships clear:

> Within the United Church of Christ, the various expressions of the church relate to each other in a covenantal manner. Each expression of the church has responsibilities and rights in relation to the others, to the end that the whole church will seek God's will and be faithful to God's mission. Decisions are made in consultation and collaboration among the various parts of the structure. As members of the Body of Christ, each expression of the church is called to honor and respect the work and ministry of each other part. Each expression of the church listens, hears, and carefully considers the advice, counsel, and requests of others. In this covenant, the various expressions of the United Church of Christ seek to walk together in all God's ways.[14]

Not insignificantly, this paragraph precedes Article 5, which contains the assurances of inviolable autonomy. Gradually, over half a century, the UCC has been, as theologian Clyde Steckel puts it, "slouching toward order," recognizing that pure autonomy never has, nor can be, an effective way of living in community. To what, then, might a still-speaking God be calling us with respect to autonomy and accountability?

I believe God may be calling this unfinished church to stop slouching, and stand up and be counted. Or to be more specific: I believe God may be calling us to develop our understanding of "accountability" as fully and completely as we have our understanding of "autonomy." The aforementioned Reuben Sheares once famously noted that in the United Church of Christ we are a people of "soft verbs." We commend and recommend, we urge, we suggest; we do not mandate, or direct, or require. Oddly enough, however, the UCC has been anything but soft-voiced and soft-verbed when it comes to accountability regarding issues of clergy and other professional misconduct—for instance, sexual harassment, child abuse, and boundary violations of various sorts. Indeed, other denominations have recognized the UCC's pioneering role in articulating where accountability lies in these matters, as well as how discipline—and reconciliation, if appropriate—are to be sought. When it comes to clergy accountability, the United Church of Christ is standing tall.

But what about the **rest** of life in our local congregations? What happens, for example, in First Church of Anytown when four of the five deacons decide that it is time for the pastor to go and then work tirelessly to ensure not only that she does go, but also that each of them is appointed to the next pastoral search committee? What happens to Second Church of Anytown, which didn't come to the last annual Conference meeting—which hasn't, in fact, sent delegates for twenty years to an annual meeting, and hasn't contributed to OCWM in anyone's memory—but which has recently been sending anti-UCC letters to the local weekly newspaper? What happens? The answer is: Probably nothing. But perhaps God is calling us to broaden our understanding of accountability. Is accountability only about pastors and other professionals in ministry—and only about their egregious abuse of individuals, at that? Might pastoral accountability also be about gross breaches of covenant with respect to the wider United Church of Christ? Even more: Are ministry professionals the only ones who share in mutual accountability?[15]

The fourth unfinished area I want to mention is ecumenical commitment. The United Church of Christ, it has often been said, is a "united and uniting" church. It is a denomination that, having been born from merger, continues to seek ways to be in visible unity with other Christian bodies. Central to the formation, the very being of the UCC is an understanding that God calls the Church to such unity not for its own sake, but for the sake of its missional activity in the world. The architects of the 1957 union posed an urgent question that may be even more urgent fifty years later: How can the churches meaningfully witness in and serve a divided world if they themselves are divided? Again, that remarkable sentence in the *Basis of Union* continues to remind inheriting generations that denominations exist not for themselves, but "as parts of that church within which each denomination is to live and labor, and, if need be, die."

In fifty years, the United Church of Christ has not abandoned this fundamental commitment; indeed, much has been accomplished ecumenically. A long-time partnership with the Christian Church (Disciples of Christ) is richer and deeper than any other American interchurch relationship short of organic merger. UCC representatives are active members and delegates in both national and global conciliar conversations, including the National and World Council of Churches, the World Alliance of Reformed Churches, and Churches Uniting in Christ (formerly the Consultation on Church Union, or COCU). For a decade the UCC has enjoyed an unfolding full communion relationship with the Presbyterian Church, USA, the Evangelical Lutheran Church in America, and the Reformed Church in America. Global partnerships, undertaken with varying degrees of intensity and seriousness, include a diverse array of churches from Chile to South Korea. And, for more than fifteen years, the United Church of Christ has had a dedicated "Minister for Ecumenical Relations," whose full-time task is to facilitate these conversations and relationships.[16]

For all this positive good, the ecumenical passion that animated the founders is **not** an animating force in many of our local congegations today, or even in our associations and conferences. There are obvious reasons for this, of course. We live in a global moment when interfaith, not inter-church, conversations seem to take precedence. Moreover, the last three or four decades have seen the rise of Christian groups—including both denominations and independent churches—whose leadership is not interested in either traditional ecumenical conversation nor cooperative work for social betterment. Nevertheless, it is a fact that many members of today's "united and uniting" Church of Christ do not even know about, let alone passionately advocate for, this ecumenical vocation.

To what might a still-speaking God be calling our "united and uniting" denomination? **I believe God may be calling this unfinished church to stretch its ecumenical muscles again.**

When delegates to the new United Church of Christ marched down the street together in Cleveland fifty years ago, they shared a sense that they were doing something momentous, something difficult. And they were. Both before and after, there have been other mergers among denominations in the United States, but arguably none that has represented a melding of quite such disparate traditions and histories, nor required so much realigning and readjusting from its members. I do not mean to dismiss the UCC's more recent ecumenical alliances as either casual or unimportant. Yet, frankly, none has demanded much from many of us—nor has any relationship excited our common passion for doing **a new thing** for the sake of the unity of Christ's church.

So perhaps God is calling us to stretch our ecumenical muscles. What might that mean? I do not pretend to have any prescription, but let me offer a personal observation to suggest the kind of direction about which, these days, I sometimes fantasize. My husband is an Episcopalian, and on Sunday mornings we go to the early Eucharist at All Saints Episcopal Church, in Wolfeboro, New Hampshire, and then across the street to First

Congregational Church, UCC, for the ten o'clock service. The Right Rev. Gene Robinson is my bishop now (at least by spousal adoption) and I have been privileged to serve on committees with his predecessor, Doug Theuner. Here is what I have observed: In New Hampshire, at least, these two denominations, whose histories and polities are so radically different, have more in common, theologically and socially, than any other two denominations I can name. What would it mean for the United Church of Christ and the Episcopal Church, USA, to be in a bi-lateral ecumenical conversation? More generally, what would it mean for the UCC to explore **any** deeper relationship that would demand we take those founding words seriously, that would challenge us to expand our theology and polity and truly change for the sake of Christian unity? Perhaps God is calling us, after fifty years, to stretch beyond our comfort zones again, to feel the cost and the joy of dying to our half-century-old self.

Now let me offer a brief final word about **tension and paradox**. This is a subject about which I have both spoken and written elsewhere, and even after fifty years it remains, I believe, a critical point of identity for the United Church of Christ. A paradox, of course, refers to apparently contradictory realities that are, nevertheless, meaningful and/or true. Christianity is full of them: the baby whose power is greater than that of kings, the death that brings life. In 1957, by virtue of our four-way merger, we became a denomination that literally built into its structures some of the traditional paradoxes of ecclesial life. Autonomy and accountability, tradition and prophetic witness, rootedness and change: In the United Church of Christ, these are not abstract theological ideas, to be pondered primarily in seminary classrooms and library cubicles. They are living commitments, codified and developed in our governing documents and struggled with daily in every setting of the church.[17] Is it theologically appropriate to change the traditional baptismal formula—Father, Son, and Holy Spirit—to render the language more gender-inclusive? How, in the light of personal witness and contemporary science, are we to interpret Biblical passages that have been used for centuries to condemn homosexual acts? When the Conference takes its stand against the "war on terror," how does my local congregation respond when many members support that war? And, not least: When will the denomination stop restructuring and declare that its institutional design is finally adequate for its mission? To what, then, might a still-speaking God be calling us, in a life of faith filled with tension and paradox?

I believe, at the end of our first fifty years, that God is calling this unfinished church to ongoing discomfort with all forms of temporal certainty and completeness. Indeed, I believe God is asking us to be certain about this: That certainty itself is God's alone. Will future members of the United Church of Christ, in their growing diversities, remain willing to live into (and out of) these paradoxes that today challenge our faith and work? If they do, it may be that God will continue to save us from all kinds of unwritten creeds and unspoken dogmatisms that can harden into false and sinful certainties, and cause us to be finished before our time and God's.

May its centennial year find this United Church of Christ—by whatever name and with whatever new structures it struggles to be faithful—resolutely unfinished, still seeking fresh light and truth from a still-speaking God.

NOTES

1. The quotation is from "The Present Crisis," written in 1845. Portions of several verses from this 17-stanza poem were included in "Once to Every Man and Nation," a popular hymn in *The Pilgrim Hymnal (#441),* but omitted in *The New Century Hymnal.*
2. In Louis H. Gunnemann, *The Shaping of the United Church of Christ* (Cleveland: United Church Press, 1977), 227-8.
3. At this writing there is no strong movement to re-write the existing *Statement of Faith* or to create a new one. Many have pointed out, however, that the SOF does not include certain contemporary concerns that were less prominent fifty years ago—for example, divine and human care for, and relationship to, the whole created world. It is not unlikely that a new Statement of Faith will emerge before the denomination's centennial.
4. *The Constitution and Bylaws, United Church of Christ,* 2001 edition, 2.
5. For the last decade, I have regularly taken informal "church of origin" surveys in gatherings of UCC members—including the Vermont Conference Annual meeting where portions of this paper were given. There, as in most settings, somewhat less than one-third of those present claimed birthright membership. Many indicated they have previously been members of, or participated in, other denominations prior to their affiliation with the UCC. A current example: In the fall, 2007 UCC History, Theology and Polity Class that I teach at Andover Newton Theological School, only 5 of 34 students (all of whom are seeking ordination or other authorization in the UCC) claimed birthright membership in the post-1957 UCC or one of its founding bodies. Ten of the remaining students claimed birthright membership in the Roman Catholic Church (the single largest birthright source for the class, with Methodism/United Methodist next, at nine). Collectively the 29 students who did not claim birthright membership in a UCC tradition participated, at one time or another, in 27 different faith groups.
6. The six papers (by Cally Rogers-Witte, J. Bennett Guess, Bernice Powell Jackson, David Schoen, Jana L. Norman, and David S. Moyer), together with three responses, were printed in the Spring, 2003 issue of *Prism.*
7. *Op.cit.* 2.
8. By "ecumenism" is usually meant a **conscious and intentional** attempt to promote unity, sharing and cooperation among different churches. I use the adjective "accidental" to suggest a kind of paradox: namely, the unconscious

and unintentional, but very real, cross-fertilization and sharing that take place when persons of widely different traditions work and worship together.

9. For example, in New England, where as many as forty percent of new UCC members are former Roman Catholics, some congregations are adopting more formal liturgies, celebrating communion more often, and experimenting with unfamiliar practices such as Ash Wednesday services and Easter vigils. This kind of mutual influence can be rich and rewarding—**and** it may someday contribute to formal ecumenical conversations. But at present, most UCC leaders have not reflected critically on the meaning and consequences of such new patterns of membership, either for the new members themselves or for the churches they are joining.

10. With few exceptions, I have rarely found **anyone** who can locate these statements, let alone summarize or paraphrase them. Should not familiarity with these statements be an assumed part of every ordinand's authorization process—and part of every new member class?

11. Of course, it is always necessary to recall that formal synodical votes concerning these and other matters are constitutionally binding on the Church only in its national setting. General Synod speaks "to, not for" the churches in their regional and local settings.

12. I would argue that these two stories pose different questions regarding the limits of inclusivity. The first raises a fundamental ecclesiological question: What does it mean to be a member—or a participant—in a UCC congregation? What role does—and should—theology play? The second raises a more functional question: What does "inclusivity" *look* like, in practice? Do some behaviors—verbal disruptiveness, "subversive" activities, or even children's consistent crying during services—suggest the need for limits on "full" inclusivity?

13. *Op. cit.*, 4.

14. *Op. cit.*, 2-3.

15. The in-progress *Manual on Church*, available from Local Church Ministries, presently on-line at the denominational website (www. ucc.org) is one step in the direction of broadening our understanding of mutual accountability. But it does not deal with the issue of accountability with respect to church members.

16. Until 1991 the denomination's chief ecumenical officer was its President, whose many responsibilities made it impossible to focus fully on ecumenical activities and relationships.

17. See the six theological affirmations, mentioned earlier, in the *Preamble to the Constitution and Bylaws*, as well as the constitutional provisions regarding autonomy and covenant.

THE NEW UNITED CHURCH OF CHRIST

Richard H. Taylor and Marjorie H. Royle

One of the great joys of the first fifty years of the life of the United Church of Christ is the new congregations that have become part of our tradition. A grand total of 1,197 new church starts and preexisting churches that were new to the UCC have entered our community in some form since 1957. Like Luke writing in the book of Acts, new churches are always a celebration of people who have heard the Gospel and covenanted to participate in the acts of God. As new churches begin, we continue a great work from all of our denominational forbears. But also, as we seek to become a multi-ethnic, multi-cultural Church, new churches reach out and form bonds with wider and wider spectrums of God's people. As we become more and more diverse we celebrate our original hope for the World, "that they may all be one."

THE EXTENT OF THIS STUDY

This study looks at all new church starts and adopted congregations new to the United Church of Christ from 1957 through 2006. Included are all churches new to the denomination appearing as full churches in *Yearbook* statistical reports for 1957 through 2006;[1] proposed churches[2] reported in the *Yearbook*[s] for 1988 through 2006;[3] additional proposed churches before 1987[4]; and new churches introduced at the 2003, 2005, and 2007 General Synods[5]. These categories total 1,197 congregations followed in this study.[6]

Where any of these congregations merged with another United Church

Richard H. Taylor is Chair of the Historical Council of the United Church of Christ. Marjorie H. Royle, Ph.D, is a religious research consultant, who previously served as Secretary for Research and Evaluation of the United Church Board for Homeland Ministries.

congregation or congregations, the resultant churches that are or have been at least partially active because of a new church beginning also have been studied.[7]

Some types of churches that might be considered as new congregations have not been included in this study. These include (1) churches formed by the merger of two or more pre-merger UCC congregations; (2) United Church of Christ congregations formed by the merger of a pre-merger UCC congregation and a congregation or congregations from outside our denominational families; (3) churches changing ethnic identity, name, location, or experiencing a major reorganization, but still constituting a continuing United Church congregation; and (4) congregations in either of the forming denominations at or just before the merger that delayed but later joined the United Church of Christ. Studies of these groups might also be of value, but are not explored here.

Prior to the 2007 General Synod the evangelism staff of Local Church Ministries (LCM) also prepared a study of new churches since 1957.[8] Their definitions for inclusion did not exactly parallel this study[9], leading to some differences in detail, although the total number of congregations new to the UCC, 1139, is similar. This study examined several issues not explored in the LCM study: That study included financial information that has not been included here. Nevertheless, results of this study support many of the conclusions they have reached, including these:

> The new churches received into the UCC during the past 50 years are a very significant and pivotal factor in our Conferences and Denomination…
>
> New church development dramatically declined after the first ten years… The decline in membership and contributions in the UCC can in part be seen as a result of the decline in new church development in the 60's, 70's, and 80's.

Although the recent increase in new church development is positive, the continued vitality and witness of the UCC in the future depends on ever increased new church development.

WHERE ARE THE NEW CHURCHES?

New Churches and population growth

One of the purposes or goals of starting new churches is to keep pace with population growth. Since 1957, churches have been started in 49 states, the District of Columbia, Puerto Rico, and Canada. To assess how well we have done with this goal nationally, state total populations from the 1960 Census were compared with the official Census estimates for 2006. During this period the net gain in population was about 120,075,000. The 1197 new congregations during this period represent almost exactly one new UCC

Church begun or adopted per 100,000-population growth. This number falls far below the number of churches that we had per 100,000 people when the Church was born which was approximately 3.8 per 100,000. Of course, net population gain hides population movements within states, changes in ethnicity and neighborhoods, age of population and a host of other factors. However, it provides at least one yardstick to see how we are doing.

The number of new churches was then compared with the net population trends in each state. (See Table 1). Much of the denomination's growth would be expected to occur in areas where we were already strong. In such

TABLES AND FIGURES

Table 1
New UCC Congregations Compared to State Population Change
1960-2006

State*	Net Population Change in 1000's, 1960-2006	Rank Absolute Growth	Pct Growth/ Decline	Number New Church Starts/ Adoptions	Rank Number New Churches	New Churches/ 100,000 population	Rank New/ 100,000
AK	444	40	196.46	5	41	1.13	23
AL	1,332	26	40.77	9	28	0.68	41
AR	1,025	32	57.39	3	45	0.29	46
AZ	4,864	5	373.58	30	13	0.62	42
CA	20,741	1	131.97	172	1	0.83	30
CO	2,999	9	170.98	32	10	1.07	25
CT	970	34	38.26	21	19	2.16	15
DC	-182	52	-23.82	3	45	-1.65	1
DE	407	41	91.26	3	45	0.74	35
FL	13,138	3	265.31	107	2	0.81	32
GA	5,421	4	137.48	19	24	0.35	45
HI	652	38	103.00	70	4	10.74	4
IA	224	46	8.12	6	35	2.68	13
ID	799	35	119.79	6	35	0.75	34
IL	2,751	10	27.29	77	3	2.80	11
IN	1,652	22	35.44	20	20	1.21	22
KS	585	39	26.85	6	35	1.03	26
KY	1,168	29	38.45	8	32	0.68	39
LA	1,031	31	31.65	4	43	0.39	43
MA	1,288	27	25.01	31	12	2.41	14
MD	2,515	13	81.10	19	22	0.80	33
ME	353	43	36.43	20	20	5.67	6
MI	2,273	15	29.06	29	16	1.28	20
MN	1,753	20	51.35	12	26	0.68	40
MO	1,523	25	35.25	27	17	1.77	18
MS	733	36	33.65	1	51	0.14	49
MT	270	44	40.00	9	28	3.33	10
NC	4,301	6	94.40	46	7	1.07	24
ND	4	50	0.63	4	43	100.00	3
NE	357	42	25.30	6	35	1.68	19
NH	708	37	116.64	6	35	0.85	29
NJ	2,658	11	43.81	23	18	0.87	28
NM	1,004	33	105.57	7	33	0.70	38
NV	2,211	16	775.79	5	41	0.23	48
NY	2,524	12	15.04	50	5	1.98	16
OH	1,772	19	18.26	48	6	2.71	12
OK	1,251	28	53.74	9	28	0.72	37

(continues on next page)

State*	Net Population Change in 1000's, 1960-2006	Rank Absolute Growth	Pct Growth/ Decline	Number New Church Starts/ Adoptions	Rank Number New Churches	New Churches/ 100,000 population	Rank New/ 100,000
OR	1,932	18	109.21	14	25	0.72	36
PA	1,122	30	9.91	43	8	3.83	8
PR	1,578	24	67.15	30	13	1.90	17
RI	209	47	24.33	7	33	3.35	9
SC	1,938	17	81.33	2	48	0.10	51
SD	101	49	14.83	6	35	5.94	5
TN	2,472	14	69.30	9	28	0.36	44
TX	13,928	2	145.39	32	10	0.23	47
UT	1,659	21	186.20	2	48	0.12	50
VA	3,676	7	92.66	30	13	0.82	31
VT	234	45	60.00	12	26	5.13	7
WA	3,543	8	124.19	33	9	0.93	27
WI	1,605	23	40.61	20	20	1.25	21
WV	-42	51	-2.26	2	48	-4.76	2
WY	185	48	56.06	0	52	0.00	52
Canada				2			
TOTAL	120,075		66.96	1197		1.00	

* The District of Columbia and Puerto Rico were included as "states." Information for the churches in Canada was not included.

states new suburbs or developments are often settled by people coming from our existing churches. Our "brand name" would already be known. Even new ethnic groups moving into such a territory would become acquainted with people from our congregations. In areas with a strong UCC presence, helpful Conference and Association programs, local support committees, even supply preachers are more readily available. Church developers in such areas should have a better grass roots sense of how populations are moving, where new areas are being settled and where growth might occur. These natural benefits are reinforced by our polity, where Associations control the policies for becoming acquainted, receiving new churches and clergy, and enforcing rules and standards. Conferences also contribute a large proportion of available funding support for new congregations, and national funding occurs in partnership with conferences.

California and Florida started the most new churches, with 172 and 107 respectively. When the rate of population growth is considered, however, their ranks dropped to 30th and 32nd. The dozen states with the highest number of new churches per 100,000 net population growth, in order, are North Dakota, Hawaii, South Dakota, Maine, Vermont, Pennsylvania, Rhode Island, Montana, Illinois, Ohio, Iowa, and Massachusetts. All of these are areas where the denomination already was strong. Responding to new ethnic growth, the Hawaii Conference founded 10.74 new churches for every 100,000 of population growth, more than ten times the national rate. In addition, new congregations have been started in areas that lost population such as the District of Columbia, and West Virginia.

On the other hand, the twelve states with the lowest number of new churches per 100,000 population growth were, in order: Alabama, Arizona, Louisiana, Tennessee, Georgia, Arkansas, Texas, Nevada, Mississippi, Utah, South Carolina, and, in last place, a state where no new congregations were formed, Wyoming. All of these would be identified as areas where we were weaker at the time of the merger. Texas, for example, even though thirty-two new congregations were added, still had a rate of 0.23 congregations per 100,000-population growth, less than a quarter of the national rate. As the national population moves to the sun belt, our Conference-centered pattern of church growth and decision-making raises problems. Creative ways are needed to move funding and leadership to where the people are. Energetic national programs are needed to make the United Church a truly national Church.

Where did the new churches come from?

Many of our new congregations are the typical intentional new church start. A Conference, sometimes prompted by a denominational agency, sees a need to reach out to a new or changing community and extend a United Church witness to that place. 787, or 65.7% of our new churches fall into this category (see Figure 1). But another large category is adoptions. Independent congregations, congregations leaving their old denomination to find one more suited to their beliefs and mission, churches seeking an ecumenical dual alignment, and local mergers of churches of several denominations seeking a new united denominational home have found

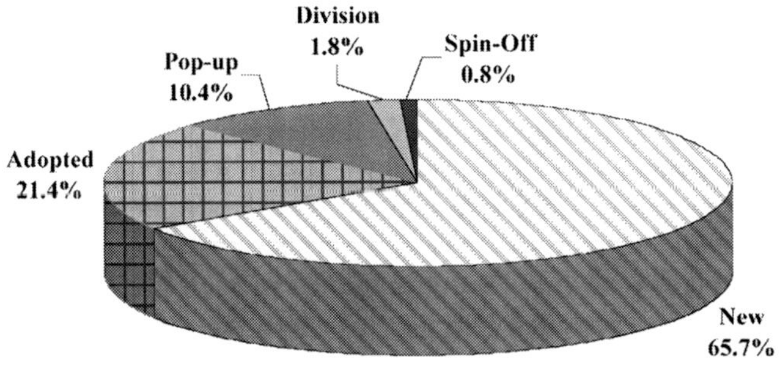

Figure 1. Types of congregations that are new to the UCC.

the United Church of Christ. 256 (21.4%) of our new Churches are such adopted congregations.

A third category, called "pop-ups," includes 124 congregations (10.4%). These are usually a group of people who have found each other and would like to form a local church, or who are in the process of doing just that, and seek out a denomination with which to affiliate. A majority of these are Asian or Pacific Islander groups that come from a sister or mission Church of ours from another land. Once they find each other, they look for their related Church family. Nearly half, however, are European or African-American or other congregations that organize on their own initiative. While the initiative to start these congregations comes from the group itself, rather than from the denomination, these churches sometimes receive some new start aid. This category represents a kind of middle ground between intentional new church starts and adoptions. It was created for this study based on subjective judgment and incomplete information, particularly in earlier years.

Two smaller categories also were identified. Some UCC Churches have begun "branch" churches at new geographic locations, which, after they are on their feet, are spun off as new congregations in full standing. Nine of these were identified. Sometimes, also, a division in a local church leads to a new congregation. Most of these appear to be a remnant committed to the UCC from congregations leaving the Church. A few are divisions of continuing churches. Twenty-one of these were identified.

In 1957, when the UCC was formed, many hoped it was the first step in further Christian unity. In this tradition, 256 independent churches and denominational churches seeking to affirm their ecumenicity (often in stronger terms than their original denomination), have found their way into the United Church. The United Church's affirmation of local church autonomy is attractive to congregations that have been independent and to congregations desiring to be more ecumenical that come from other denominations with local autonomy. Our liturgical breadth from free-spirited to more formal or liturgical builds no barrier to churches with various worship styles. Our theological diversity can encourage congregations that find the same breadth among their own people. Our desire to address certain social issues engages churches that have been similarly active. Our desire to include people often shunned by other faith communities is often a welcoming star to churches engaged on the same journey. Our long-term association with certain ethnic and national communities at home and abroad often provides a natural fit.

These new congregations came from several different backgrounds. Many of them were from the Council of Community Churches. Another smaller group were Christian churches from the Unitarian and Universalist traditions. Some of these congregations, particularly those from Baptist traditions and from our partner denomination, the Christian Church (Disciples of Christ), hoped to maintain a dual denominational alignment.

Throughout the history of the UCC, dual alignments or federated churches have been common, representing 117 or 10% of all new congregations. Only about half of these (51%) were congregations of another denomination seeking to affiliate with the UCC, while most of the remainder (44%) were begun as churches relating to two denominations. The most common denominational affiliations of congregations participating in these dual relationships were American and other Baptists and the Christian Church (Disciples of Christ). However, many other denominations were involved, including, in recent years, the Metropolitan Community Churches.

The Blake – Pike proposal (1960) that led to the formation in 1962 of the Consultation on Church Union (COCU)—now Churches Uniting in Christ, heightened expectations for a broader united church. A number of the new congregations, particularly in the years that followed, were dually, triply, and sometimes four and five denomination aligned. Twenty-five such congregations were identified in this study, half of them being intentional new church starts. Almost all of them (10/12) were founded in the 15 years following COCU's formation. Most often our partners in these multiple alignments were the Presbyterian Church, U.S.A, the United Methodist Church, and the Christian Church (Disciples of Christ), although many other Protestant denominations were represented. At the same time denominational churches about to move or change ethnicity were also often encouraged to seek endorsement and dual alignment from other mainline denominations. Of course, the new super-united Church never appeared. In the meantime many congregations had significant difficulty maintaining relationships to several denominations, their priorities and expectations. As a result many of these multi-aligned churches, often with the arrival of new leadership, retreated to two or one denominational affiliation. A proportion of the new churches shown in this study as withdrawn are not so much congregations disagreeing with denominational policy as they are ecumenically inclined churches adjusting their denominational affiliations.

Are our new churches surviving?

Are our new churches succeeding? Do they last? Do they grow? While we believe that all work done on God's behalf produces good fruit, we do hope that churches succeed. How do we measure growth? Many UCC believers would hope that 100% of our Churches last over time and grow to significant size. But that is far from potential reality.

Clay Price from the Baptist General Convention of Texas indicated in a recent conversation that, while that convention starts "two hundred to two hundred and fifty churches a year," in "five years, 40% of them will be gone." In other words, they expect only 60% of their new starts to last longer than five years. Other denominations report similar percentages. The survival rate for all of the Churches founded in the UCC in the last fifty years, some of them now fifty years old, is 63.3%. Others have merged into continuing congregations. Many denominations would expect a much lower survival rate over such an extended period of time.

Because proposed congregations do not submit *Yearbook,* reports and all active congregations do not always report membership statistics, we will combine information from congregations reporting membership and those not reporting. For all new congregations, 633 are active and reported 2006 membership in the 2007 *Yearbook,* totaling 127,167 members. Another 125 congregations are alive but did not report membership, for a total of 758 of 1,197 congregations, or 63%, still active. Therefore, in 2007, new congregations represent considerably more than a minimum of 127, 167 members.

Another way that new congregations survive is by merging with other congregations. Information by race/ethnicity for the 40 new congregations and the new or older congregations with which they merged reveals an increase of 8,855 members.

The second half of the story, presented in Table 3, is what happened to congregations that are no longer active in the UCC. For all churches, 51 of 1,197 or 4.3% merged with other UCC congregations (40 of which are still active) reveals an increase of 8,855 members, 109 or 9.1% withdrew from the denomination, and 279 or 23.3% closed. Thus, the majority of losses of new churches have been closings rather than withdrawals.

Table 3

Non-Surviving Churches by Racial/Ethnic Group

Ethnic Group	Total Number	Merged Churches	Percent	Withdrew Churches	Percent	Closed Churches	Percent
African-American	118	3	2.5	10	8.5	26	22.0
African-Caribbean	7	0		0		3	42.9
European	730	38	5.2	68	9.3	191	26.2
Hispanic*	87	4	4.6	9	10.3	23	26.4
Multi-Ethnic	20	0		0		3	15.0
Native American	4	0		0		3	75.0
Asian-Pacific	231	6	2.6	22	9.5	30	13.0
TOTAL	1,197	51	4.3	109	9.1	279	23.3%

* The United Evangelical Church of Puerto Rico voted to withdraw from the United Church in 2006. However, all full standing Puerto Rican churches were listed in the 2007 United Church Yearbook awaiting a confirming action from the 2007 General Synod.

ARE WE BECOMING MORE DIVERSE?

Ethnic identity

Are our new churches helping fulfill our goal to become a multi-racial and multi-cultural Church? The four major historic strands of the United Church of Christ derived from British and German European roots. Those ethnic identities are still the largest within today's Church. Nevertheless, long before 1957 some of these traditions had encountered native American peoples. Congregations were founded serving a wide variety of Indian nations. African-American members were found in colonial congregations and uniquely Black congregations began in the early nineteenth century.

Waves of European immigration led to starting new churches among residents from almost every language-cultural group in western and central Europe. Hispanic congregations were unique among European language groups, as most congregations were in or represented immigration from Latin America rather than directly from Spain. The first fruits of foreign missionary work to significantly foster churches in North America was immigration from American Board-initiated churches in Armenia. The Hawaiian Evangelical Association, another fruit of American Board work, brought many native Hawaiian congregations into our cultural mix.

However, growth from other parts of the world before 1957 was more limited. The largest groups from other lands were Chinese and Japanese congregations found both in Hawaii and on the mainland. There was one Assyrian Church. Filipino churches had begun in Hawaii before the First World War. By the mid 1950s and early 1960s they were often leaders in merging into multi-national and multi-cultural congregations.

A few other ethnic-cultural groups were relatively new to the merging Churches. The only immigrant African or Caribbean Church at the start of 1957 was a Cape Verdean Church that had gained standing in 1949. The first two Samoan congregations both joined the Hawaii Conference in 1956.

One of the most exciting things about "the new United Church of Christ" has been the significant growth in congregations with new ethnic identities. 730 churches, or 61.0%, of our new congregations began as predominantly general European English-speaking churches. A few with specific European identities have joined us, such as German (six churches, including the majority of congregations in the colonial-era Pennsylvania Schwenkfelder Church), Hungarian (9 churches), and Armenian (1 church). In addition, traditional constituencies such as African-American (117 churches, 9.8%), Hispanic (87 churches, 7.3%), Native American (4 churches, 0.3%), and overall Pacific Islander and Asian (231 churches, 19.3%) have grown significantly since 1957.

However, new immigrant African and Caribbean churches have also joined the denomination (7 churches, 0.6%), including Haitian (3 churches),

Sudanese (2), Liberian (1), and Ewe (1). These new groups reflect the changing demographics of United States immigration.

Spectacular growth has occurred in specific Pacific Islander and Asian groups. Some of the new churches continue growth in older families such as Chinese (6 churches on the mainland), Japanese (5 churches in Hawaii, one on the mainland), and native Hawaiian (3 in Hawaii). Samoan has been the fastest growing Pacific constituency (31 in Hawaii, 77 on the mainland), while Filipino churches have expanded to the mainland (3 in Hawaii, 30 on the mainland). Other entirely new PAAM ethnic identity churches include Korean (3 in Hawaii, 21 on the mainland), Taiwanese-Formosan (4

Table 4
Racial/Ethnic Composition of New Churches by State

State	Race/Ethnicity						Total
	African/ Afr. Amer	European	Hispanic	Multi-Ethnic	Native American	Pacific/ Asian	
AK	-	3	-	-	-	2	5
AL	3	5	-	1	-	-	9
AR	1	-	-	-	-	2	3
AZ	-	26	1	-	-	3	30
CA	6	80	5	5	-	76	172
Canada	-	1	-	-	-	1	2
CO	2	26	1	-	-	3	32
CT	3	7	8	-	-	3	21
DC	3	-	-	-	-	-	3
DE	1	1	-	1	-	-	3
FL	6	94	5	1	-	1	107
GA	8	9	-	-	-	2	19
HI	-	6	-	-	-	64	70
IA	-	6	-	-	-	-	6
ID	-	6	-	-	-	-	6
IL	10	47	8	2	-	10	77
IN	2	17	1	-	-	-	20
KS	1	4	-	-	-	1	6
KY	-	8	-	-	-	-	8
LA	1	2	-	1	-	-	4
MA	1	16	7	2	-	5	31
MD	5	12	-	-	-	2	19
ME	-	20	-	-	-	-	20
MI	5	20	1	-	-	3	29
MN	1	10	-	-	1	-	12
MO	2	21	2	-	-	2	27
MS	-	1	-	-	-	-	1
MT	-	9	-	-	-	-	9
NC	16	28	2	-	-	-	46
ND	1	1	-	-	2	-	4
NE	-	6	-	-	-	-	6
NH	-	5	-	-	-	1	6
NJ	1	16	1	-	-	5	23
NM	-	7	-	-	-	-	7
NV	-	3	-	-	-	2	5
NY	10	23	7	-	-	10	50
OH	5	38	1	2	-	2	48
OK	1	6	-	-	-	2	9
OR	1	10	-	-	-	3	14
PA	12	24	3	2	-	2	43
PR	-	-	30	-	-	-	30

State	Race/Ethnicity African/ Afr. Amer	European	Hispanic	Multi-Ethnic	Native American	Pacific/ Asian	Total
RI	-	4	1	-	-	2	7
SC	-	2	-	-	-	-	2
SD	2	3	-	-	1	-	6
TN	1	8	-	-	-	-	9
TX	3	19	2	1	-	7	32
UT	-	1	-	-	-	1	2
VA	8	17	-	2	-	3	30
VT	-	12	-	-	-	-	12
WA	1	20	1	-	-	11	33
WI	2	18	-	-	-	-	20
WV	-	2	-	-	-	-	2
WY	-	-	-	-	-	-	-
Total	125	730	87	20	4	231	1197

on the mainland), Tongan (1 in Hawaii), Laotian (2 mainland), Indonesian (1 mainland), and South Indian, including Malayalam and Tamil (14 on the mainland). Also new are four Micronesian groups including Marshallese (5 in Hawaii, 7 on the mainland), Kosraen (3 in Hawaii), Pohnepeian (2 in Hawaii, 1 on the mainland), and Chuukese (4 in Hawaii, 2 on the mainland). Some Pacific-Asian congregations have a multi-national, multi-cultural constituency (4 in Hawaii, 1 on the mainland).

Although congregations from different ethnic groups generally are located in areas of major migration, such as Asian and Pacific Islanders in California or Hispanic congregations in Chicago or New York City, they are also found throughout the United States, as can be seen in Table 4. For example, an Indonesian congregation is located in New Hampshire, Sudanese congregations were founded in North and South Dakota and Micronesian congregations were founded in Kansas, Missouri, Arkansas, and Oklahoma.

The proportion of new churches that were begun as predominantly European has declined markedly over the five decades, as can be seen in Figure 2 and Table 6. While 90.6% of new churches in the first decade (1957-1966) were European in background, only 34.4% were European in the most recent decade (1997-2006). Being similar ethnically to most existing UCC churches, European churches are the most likely to merge with other United Church of Christ congregations. Their average size hovers near the general average. However, as the denomination as a whole adopted the goal of being multi-racial, multi-cultural, open and affirming, and accessible to all, some of these predominantly European congregations (20 churches, 1.7%) in recent years have described themselves as multi-ethnic and intentionally tried to incorporate people from various racial and ethnic backgrounds. Our information is not complete enough to indicate how well these congregations are doing towards achieving that goal.

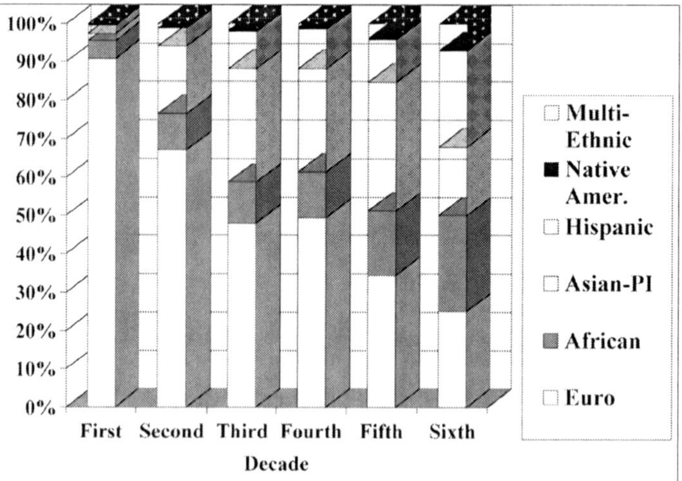

Figure 2. Changes by decade in racial/ethnic new churches.

Table 6
Changes in Racial/Ethnic Composition of New Churches by Decade

Racial/ Ethnic Group	Decade												Total	
	1		2		3		4		5		6			
	N	%	N	%	N	%	N	%	N	%	N	%	N	%
African-American	18	4.8	16	9.4	18	10.1	22	11.8	37	14.5	7	25.0	118	9.9
Afro/ Caribbean	0	0.0	0	0.0	1	0.6	0	0.0	6	2.3	0	0.0	7	0.6
Euro	343	90.7	114	67.1	86	48.0	92	49.5	88	34.4	7	25.0	730	61.0
Hispanic	8	2.1	8	4.7	17	9.5	19	10.2	28	10.9	7	25.0	87	7.3
Multi-Ethnic	1	0.3	2	1.2	3	1.7	2	1.1	10	3.9	2	7.1	20	1.7
Native American	1	0.3	0	0.0	1	0.6	1	0.5	1	0.4	0	0.0	4	0.3
PacificIsl./ Asian	7	1.9	30	17.6	53	29.6	50	26.9	86	33.6	5	17.9	231	19.3

Although the Pacific Islander and Asian category might be considered the fourth largest ethnic group in the country (following European, Hispanic, and African-American) it has ranked second among new Church starts. In the first decade, these congregations were less than 2% of new starts; they have risen to 33.6% of the new starts in the fifth decade. Asian Pacific churches have also had the highest survival rate of the larger ethnic groups, with 74.9% of churches still alive (see Table 2). While their average church size (121) remains lower, this may suggest the isolation of some new Pacific and Asian communities. We have been very blessed by the settlement in America of people from our sister churches in Samoa, Micronesia, and India. The United Church is probably the largest Protestant or Christian denomination among some Pacific Island groups in America.

Among Pacific Islander and Asian congregations, Native Hawaiian churches were more likely to begin as intentional new starts, while Chinese and Asian Indian congregations were more likely to be adopted and other Pacific Islander and Asian congregations often organized and then looked to a denomination with name recognition in their home country with whom to affiliate. In addition to the importance of historic ties with churches in many Asian countries, opening full communion with the Presbyterian Church in the Republic of Korea has played some role in developing Korean congregations in the United States.

New African-American congregations were 4.8% of our new churches during the height of the Civil Rights movement in our first decade. They have grown to be 14.5% of the new churches in the fifth decade. Of the major ethnic groups they have the lowest percentage of churches withdrawing from the denomination (see Table 3). They also have by far the highest average membership of our new churches, 534 per church, compared to an overall average of 201.

Many might speculate that the large average African-American Church size among new churches is brought about by two widely known congregations: Trinity in Chicago and Victory in Stone Mountain, GA. They truly lead the way. But even with their data removed, the remaining 52 African-American congregations for whom membership size is known have 14,924 members, an average of 287. This is still significantly larger than the current average UCC congregation, is 40% higher than new churches as a whole, and is about 50% higher than any other ethnic group. We obviously have many highly gifted and successful church planters and ministers in the African-American community. Hopefully, they will be able to mentor and train more leaders, who will receive strong denominational support for additional new starts in opening fields.

The Hispanic community is the fastest growing major ethnic group in the country. Initiatives to start new Hispanic Churches were increased after 1987 when General Synod XVI adopted "a proposal for action" in response to concerns raised by Hispanic members. This proposal called for all settings of the denomination to intentionally address the needs of Hispanics. New Hispanic church starts rose from 2.1% of the new churches in our first decade to 10.9% in the last decade.

Over a third (34.5%) of our new Hispanic Churches were in Puerto Rico, where most of our Hispanic members continued to live. In Puerto Rico, where a strong tradition exists of congregations starting other congregations in nearby towns, survival rates for new congregations are extremely high, 90.0% (see Table 7). The withdrawal in 2006 of the Iglesia Evangélica Unida de Puerto Rico (the Puerto Rico Conference) has been a loss to the entire denomination. While immediate issues have influenced that decision, paternalism and general American colonial influences may have prepared the stage for that event.

Table 7
Hispanic Congregations on the Mainland and in Puerto Rico

Category and Measure	Mainland	PR before withdrawal	Total	PR after withdrawal	Total
Total Churches	57	30	87	30	87
Alive w/members	16	23	39	0	16
Total members	972	1,575	2,547	0	972
Avg.Membership	61	68	65	0	61
Alive/no member data	12	4	16	0	12
Total % Alive	49.1%	90.0%	63.2%	0	32.2%
Churches merged	2	2	4	2	4
% Merged	3.5%	6.7%	4.6%	6.7%	4.6%
Churches withdrew	5	0	5	27	32
% Withdrew	8.8%	0%	5.7%	90.0%	36.8%
Churches closed	22	1	23	1	23
% Closed	38.6%	3.3%	26.4%	3.3%	26.4%
Living Merged Churches	2	2	4	0	2
Total members	304	277	581	0	304
Avg.Membership	152	138	145	0	152

On the mainland, only 49.1% of our new Hispanic Churches have survived, lower than any of the other four major ethnic groups. The average size for continuing congregations is also 61, the lowest for any of the major ethnic groups. New congregations have been more likely to survive in the Chicago area and urban areas in the northeast where there was already a Hispanic UCC presence and several congregations were nearby than in areas in the south and west where they were the only Hispanic UCC for many miles, even though many Hispanics lived in the area. Many of the factors that have helped congregations of other ethnic groups prosper have worked against the success of mainland Hispanic congregations. Hispanic immigrants other than Puerto Ricans come from countries that do not have a strong Protestant tradition with United Church name recognition. If they are familiar at all with Protestants, it is with Pentecostals. In addition, Hispanic immigrants are often among the poorest, with few financial resources to contribute to a new congregation.

Church membership itself may be a foreign concept to Hispanic immigrants. Many are former Roman Catholics who may be hesitant to become members of a Protestant congregation, even if they are active participants. Even the concept of becoming a member of a church is unfamiliar to Roman Catholics who automatically become part of a geographic parish when they move. Finally, those who are undocumented or those who are fleeing from political unrest may be particularly hesitant to sign their names to join an organization.

Identification and development of leadership, especially clergy leadership, has been difficult. Unlike Asian and Pacific Islander immigrants, clergy and lay leaders from among these immigrants are not likely to have a UCC or even Protestant church background, and new church developers must teach their leaders new information, roles and skills while learning them themselves. UCC Hispanic congregations both on the mainland and in Puerto Rico have provided the strongest leaders. Clergy from other denominations or from other Latin American countries often have had significant theological differences from those common in the UCC, which has resulted in their leaving the churches or taking the churches with them to other denominations.

The success of the Iglesia Evangélica Unida de Puerto Rico in growing new congregations and the success on the mainland in Chicago and cities in the northeast provide some clues for achieving greater success in establishing new Hispanic congregations elsewhere on the mainland. Developing new churches with the help of existing churches, growing new clergy and lay leaders from within existing UCC Hispanic congregations, and ensuring that new congregations have access to denominational resources in Spanish all are important strategies. Sources of resources might include those used in other congregations, as well as new ones developed by the national offices. In addition, our partner churches including the Congregational Church of Mexico, the Evangelical and Reformed Church in Honduras, and the Pentecostal Church of Chile, as well as former colleagues in the Iglesia Evangélica Unida de Puerto Rico could be encouraged to share their resources, where appropriate, including trained pastors, as well as names of immigrants to the US who might be linked with new and existing Hispanic congregations. In addition, we might develop resources and train clergy and lay leaders jointly with these partners, thereby enriching both.

Clearly, we are being blessed by immigration from lands where our missionaries founded churches (such as Micronesia), and where our sister churches founded missions (such as the London Missionary Society in Samoa). These blessings also extend to churches formed or strengthened by immigrants from United Churches that would identify with our name, and also include some congregations from our earlier missionary endeavors (such as the United Church of Christ in the Philippines, the United Church of Christ in Japan, and the Church of South India.) We rejoice that strong ecumenical ties exist with the Churches in these homelands. We can learn from them if and where people from their churches are settling in the United States. We can potentially help each other with pastoral education, common resources for evangelism, church school curricula, and other areas, and in understanding and addressing specific and more universal social and humanitarian issues and needs.

HOW HAS CHURCH PLANTING CHANGED OVER THE DECADES?

As the LCM study reports, the first decade of the UCC's life was the era of church planting, in the UCC as well as in other mainline Protestant denominations. No decades since that time have approached the level of new and adopted churches, as can be seen in Table 8.

Table 8
New Congregations by Decade

Decade	Number of New Congregations	Number of New Congregations, Excluding Proposed and Synod Only
1957-66	378	376
1967-76	170	170
1977-86	180	174
1987-96	186	154
1997-2006	255	139
2007 (-2016)	28	0

Several related changes in how new congregations are incorporated into the denomination have affected new church development and how it must be studied. Historically, whenever a congregation decided it was ready to formalize its relationship with the denomination, it requested membership and its application was voted upon. If approved, it became part of the denomination and was listed in the *Yearbook.* In some conferences or at some times, new congregations were listed at an early point in their organization, while in others, they were encouraged to wait to apply for full status and *Yearbook* listing until they were thriving with at least 100 members. Beginning with the 1989 *Yearbook*, a special section was created to list proposed congregations so that they would receive denominational mailings and their information would be available to individuals seeking a UCC in their area. In a parallel development, as conference or association Church in Ministry Committees formalized their procedures, many created a process for "Churches in Formation" paralleling the "In-Care" process for candidates for ministry. The UCC *Manual on Church* (Draft 2, January 2005) provides guidelines for this process of Establishing Covenant, which it suggests may take two years. These developments created a de-facto new category of congregations, "Proposed Churches." The practice of reporting and celebrating new and proposed churches at each of the last three General Synods enhanced this category.

This practice affects the way new churches are counted. While the number of new congregations has increased in the last decade and, if present rates continue, will be expected to increase in the current decade, most of this increase is due to the inclusion of these Proposed Churches, as can be seen in the last column of Table 8. When the proposed congregations that have not yet attained full standing are removed, the number of new congregations has continued to decrease. This lower number is probably an underestimate, however, because some of these congregations are worshiping bodies with a nucleus of people and may well have been included as full congregations if the Proposed Church option did not exist.

This new practice is not used uniformly throughout the church, and has been implemented in different places at different times. For example, some conferences, including New York and Missouri/MidSouth, have listed few or no congregations as Proposed in the *Yearbook*. Others, including Central Atlantic, Central Pacific, and Northern California, have designated most or all of their new churches as Proposed. In Conferences that list some but not all congregations as Proposed, congregations started more recently and ones that are started intentionally are more likely to be listed, while adoptions, those that are dually aligned, or pop-ups are less likely to be listed. Information was not available on what new congregations were guided through a Churches in Formation process rather than admitted directly, although the overlap is probably large.

This long gestation period runs counter to our historic traditions where churches moved quickly into full fellowship. That way they received votes and influential power in associations and similar bodies. Since 1997, 40% of our new churches have been assigned to the *Yearbook* proposed lists and presumably to the Churches in Formation process. Those that have moved to full standing spent an average of 2.5 years as proposed congregations, about the time that the *Manual on Church* recommends. Those that are still on the list have spent an average of 4 years there. Four congregations have been listed as proposed congregations for 12 years. In both of these categories (moved to full standing, still proposed), the congregations spending the highest average times on the proposed list have been Hispanic or Pacific and Asian. This may indicate that congregations with different cultures or languages are slowed down in the process. As one of our old traditions suggested:

> When a company of believers purpose to gather into church fellowship, it is requisite for their safer proceeding & the maintaining of the communion of churches, that they signify their intent unto the neighbor churches, walking according unto the order of the Gospel, & desire their presence, & help, & right hand of fellowship which *they ought regularly to give unto them,* when there is no just cause excepting against their proceedings.[10] (Italics added).

Sources of new congregations have remained quite similar across the decades, as can be seen in Table 9. The first and third decades had the largest percentages of intentional starts even though the numbers started in the third decade were low. Pop-ups are a recent phenomenon, although, because this category is the least objective and based on additional knowledge of the congregations, the increase may reflect may reflect more complete information in recent years. In the fifth decade, adoptions increased to the level of the first two decades, after dropping in the third and fourth decades. The little information available from one year of the sixth decade suggests that this trend is continuing. The publicity surrounding General Synod XXV's statement on marriage equality and recent disparate issues and directions in some other denominations may be fueling a new wave of adoptions in the months and years ahead.

Table 9
Sources of New Congregations by Decade

	Source of Congregation									
	Adoptions		Pop-ups		Intentional New		Spin-offs		Divisions	
	N	%	N	%	N	%	N	%	N	%
1957-66	84	22.2	9	2.4	280	74.1	2	0.5	3	0.8
1967-76	42	24.7	13	7.6	109	64.1	0	0.0	6	3.5
1977-86	29	16.1	12	6.7	132	73.3	2	1.1	5	2.8
1987-96	33	17.7	27	14.5	118	63.4	4	2.2	4	2.2
1997-2006	58	22.7	55	21.6	138	54.1	1	0.4	3	1.2
2007 (-16)	10	35.7	8	28.6	10	35.7	0	0.0	0	0.0
Total	256	21.4	124	10.4	787	65.7	9	0.8	21	1.8

MEGA-CHURCHES

The "mega-church" seems to be a creation of the last several decades. Cathedrals, though, have been around for centuries. While there were large churches in our traditions in the seventeenth and eighteenth centuries, both the covenantal tradition and the Cambridge Platform tended to keep churches limited to the number of people that could conveniently meet together at one time. Nevertheless, the modern ease of transportation, as well as desires for broad services and highly effective leadership have empowered an age of large churches. While this may have had little effect on much of the United Church, it is part of our new churches. Indeed eight of the fifteen largest congregations in the United Church are new to the denomination in the last fifty years. These include the four largest congregations: Trinity Church in Chicago, Victory Church in Stone Mountain, Georgia, First Community Church in Columbus, Ohio, and the Cathedral of Hope in Dallas.

WHAT FACTORS AFFECT SURVIVAL?

The Life-Span of New Congregations

Starting a new congregation is not easy, and many do not survive. Is there a critical period in a congregation's life after which survival is more likely? Because information on all new starts and adoptions was available for up to 50 years for some congregations, this question could be addressed. To do so, survival graphs were developed for all new, adopted, and pop-up congregations that joined the UCC between 1957 and 1987, so that all would have had the opportunity to survive for at least 20 years. Although this method describes survival, it does so only for churches that were started in the past, using older church development goals and assumptions and a racial/ethnic mix of congregations founded 20 to 50 years ago. The picture obtained from these congregations will not necessarily be the same for congregations founded today.

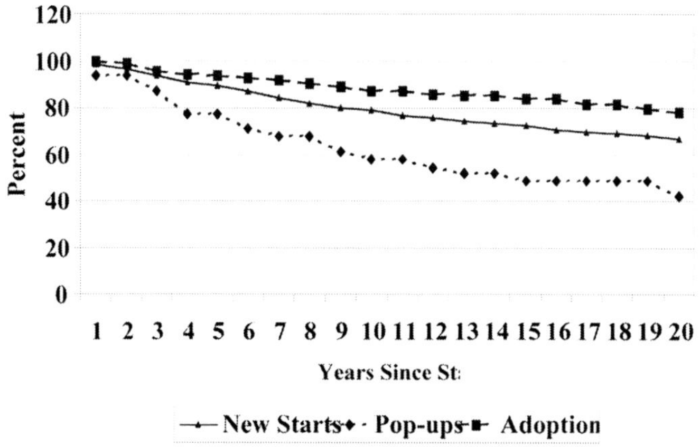

Figure 3. 20-year survival rates of all new churches (churches founded before 1987 only).

The vast majority of the 727 congregations started or adopted before 1987 were still alive in 2007 (see Figure 3). Of the adopted congregations, 78% were still active 20 years after they joined the UCC. Two thirds of the intentional new church starts were still active, but only 42% of the pop-ups were still active. In each case, decreases were greater in the first decade than the second. For intentional new starts, 2% to 3% were lost every year for about the first 10 years, when the rate of loss decreased a little to 0.5% to 1%. For adoptions, the rates of loss were a little smaller, and nearly leveled off in the second decade. For pop-ups, the losses began immediately and dropped by 4% per year for the first 10 years, and again dropped off to 1 to 2% per year in the second decade.

Because the first ten years seem important for survival, the 291 churches started or adopted before 1997 that closed, merged, or withdrew in those first 10 years were examined more closely. For each year, the number in each of these categories was calculated. Results for intentional new church starts are shown in Figure 4. Closure was by far the most typical outcome, peaking at 4 years. A few congregations merged after several years, and fewer still withdrew.

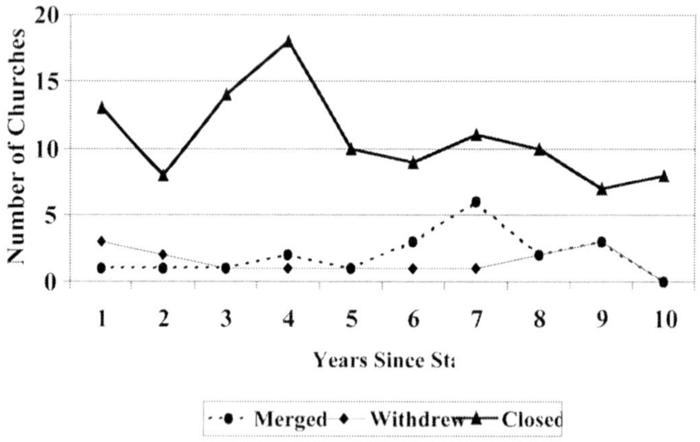

Figure 4. Losses of intentional new church starts in the first ten years (churches founded before 1997 only).

For adoptions, the graph (not shown) was essentially flat, with 1 or 2 congregations being lost each year. Very few congregations were lost at all, and merger, withdrawal and closure were about equally common reasons for the losses. For pop-ups, (not shown), closures were the most common reason, and most closures took place in the first few years. No pop-up merged with another UCC congregation, and withdrawals were minimal. One concern that is sometimes expressed is that adopted or pop-up congregations will join the denomination in order to obtain resources, and then withdraw later because of underlying differences in theology. No evidence was found that this is occurring.

Differences in Survival and Growth by the Congregation's Origins

The information available allowed examination of several factors that might be expected to have an impact on whether a new congregation survives and grows. Population change in various regions of the country is one such factor that has already been discussed. Others include whether survival and growth were better in some decades than others, whether pre-existing congregations or those that organized themselves and then asked to join the UCC were more likely to survive than those that were intentionally planted, and whether affiliation with more than one denomination helped or hindered survival. Racial/ethnic composition, regional demographics or conference resources, policies and procedures may all affect survival. Each of these factors will be examined.

Congregations that had some pre-existing history, as an independent body, as part of another denomination, or as part of another UCC congregation all had a survival advantage, as can be seen in Table 10. After ten or more years, about 63% of these congregations were still alive and in the UCC, while only 54.5% of intentional new starts were still alive in the UCC. Pop-ups fared even less well, with only 32.8% still alive and in the UCC. Spin-offs, adoptions, and pop-ups were more likely to withdraw from the denomination than intentional new starts, and pop-ups were more likely to close than intentional new starts. These results suggest that the efforts put into selecting good locations for new churches and the resources provided them seem to be significant in their eventual success.

Because they came into the denomination as more mature churches, adopted churches were also larger, with a mean of 269 members, while intentional new starts had a mean of 196 members and spin-offs had a mean of 188 members after at least 10 years of growth. Divisions were the smallest, with a mean of 64 members, while pop-ups had a mean of 122 members.

Table 10
Current Status by Sources of New Congregations
(From Those Started in the First Four Decades)

	Current Status of Congregation									
	Alive		Proposed		Merged		Withdrew		Closed	
Source	N	%	N	%	N	%	N	%	N	%
Adoptions	118	62.8	0	0.0	8	4.3	39	20.7	23	12.2
Pop-ups	20	32.8	2	3.3	0	0.0	12	19.7	27	44.3
Intentional New Starts	349	54.5	3	0.5	39	6.1	41	6.4	190	29.8
Spin-offs	5	62.5	0	0.0	0	0.0	3	37.5	0	0.0
Divisions	12	66.7	0	0.0	0	0.0	2	11.1	4	22.2
Total	504	55.2	5	0.5	47	5.1	97	10.6	244	26.7

Regional Geographic Differences

Depending on how success is defined, different areas of the country were more successful than others at starting or adopting new congregations (see table 11). If success is defined as starting churches that are still active at least 10 years after founding, Puerto Rico was most successful by far, at 84%, followed by New York at 72%, Rocky Mountain and Southwest and Northern New England (Maine, New Hampshire and Vermont) at 68%, and Central Atlantic at 66%. Southern, the Sunbelt (Southeast and South Central), were least successful. Illinois, Ohio, and Pennsylvania (the four Pennsylvania conferences and Calvin Synod) grew the largest churches. Looking at the back door, the Rivers area (Illinois South, Indiana-Kentucky,and Missouri/MidSouth) (4%), Northern California (5%), the Plains (Iowa, Kansas, Nebraska, the Dakotas, and Montana) (6%), and Rocky Mountain/Southwest and the Sunbelt (Southeast and South Central) had the fewest new churches withdraw, and Puerto Rico (0.4%) and Northern New England (6%) had the fewest new churches close. In addition, but not shown in the table, Illinois led in mergers with 10 or 16%, Southern California and Pennsylvania were second with 7 and 3 or 9% each. Of course, mergers are more likely in areas where more UCC congregations are available with which to merge.

Table 11
Church Planting Success by Geographical Area
(for Congregations Started in the First Four Decades)

Conference/ Group	Currently Active Churches		Churches Withdrawing		Churches Closing		Membership[a]	
	Number	Percent	Number	Percent	Number	Percent	Mean	Median
Southern	18	41%	6	14%	17	39%	94	74
Sunbelt (SC, SE)	19	43%	3	7%	22	50%	140	118
Northwest (PNW, CPC)	19	46%	4	10%	15	37%	87	90
Plains (IA, KS, NE, SD, ND, MT)	16	48%	2	6%	13	39%	171	155
Ohio	19	48%	5	12%	14	35%	452	150
Illinois	30	49%	7	12%	14	23%	526	84
So. Cal.	39	52%	12	16%	17	23%	139	117
Great Lakes (MI, MN, WI)	31	54%	8	14%	15	26%	220	151
Penn. (PC, PNE, PSE, PW, Calvin)	18	54%	5	15%	7	21%	316	170
No. Cal.	34	55%	3	5%	21	34%	128	104
Rivers (ILSO, IK, MOMidSo	29	59%	2	4%	16	33%	183	194
Hawaii	26	60%	8	19%	8	19%	158	116
Florida	60	63%	6	6%	28	30%	262	178
So. New Eng (CT, MA, RI)	27	63%	7	16%	8	19%	112	82
Central Atlantic	29	66%	4	9%	9	20%	227	141
No. New Eng. (ME, NH, VT)	22	68%	6	19%	2	6%	89	49
RockyMt/SW	40	68%	4	7%	12	23%	253	172
New York	28	72%	5	13%	5	13%	129	108
Puerto Rico	16[b]	84%	0	0%	1	0.4%	73	62

[a] Because numbers of active churches were small in some groups, the median as well as the mean is displayed to minimize the effect of a few particularly large (or small) congregations.

[b] This analysis included PR churches as active churches, rather than withdrawing because these congregations remain active in the IEUPR.

Although these regional and conference differences are interesting, they show no clear commonalities. That is, states within a region do not show the same patterns of success, nor do conferences in which the UCC is relatively strong or weak. The factors that lead to success in sustaining new congregations may be more on a local or associational level than a conference or regional one. These could include skill in finding good locations, choosing skilled clergy leadership, and garnering support for the new congregations from other area congregations.

How All These Factors Interact

Time since founding, type of new congregation, ethnicity, and area of the country all affect whether a new congregation survives and grows. To understand the relative effect of these various factors, a technique called multiple regression was used to predict survival and church size from these four factors. In this technique, the effects of one factor are controlled for when examining the next factor. For example, one would expect that congregations founded in the 60s would be larger than those founded in the 90s because they have had longer to grow. The multiple regression analysis accounted for the effect of time since founding before examining the effect of the type of new start, adoption, pop-up, true new start, or other. Then those factors were taken into account before examining the effect of race/ethnicity, and it was taken into account before examining the effect of geography.

When survival was examined, time since founding had an effect, but actually a very small one. Congregations founded earlier were more likely to be still alive, probably because the late 50's and early 60's were the time of the church growth boom. Adoptions were much more likely to survive than pop-ups, with new starts in the middle. When these factors were taken into account, Asian and Pacific Islander congregations were more likely to survive than mixed ethnic congregations, which were more likely to survive than African- and Euro-American congregations. Mainland Hispanic congregations were the least likely to survive. Finally, when ethnicity was also taken into account, congregations in Florida, the Rocky Mountain/Southwest area, and New York were much more likely to survive than others, while those in the Pacific Northwest, Southeast, South Central and the Southern Conference were less likely to survive. Although these differences were statistically significant, they were not large. Taken together, they explained about 7% of the likelihood of survival, with factors including the demographics of the location, the skills of the pastor, and the resources available probably explaining much more.

The picture for congregational size is similar. This analysis included only the congregations that survived. Time since founding explained less of the difference in size than it did in survival, less than 1%. Once again, adoptions were larger than planned new starts which were larger than pop-ups. African-American congregations were much larger than others, with Asian and Pacific Islander and mainland Hispanic congregations being smaller. Finally, when other factors were taken into account, congregations in Illinois (led by Trinity UCC) were larger and those in New York, Southeast, South Central and the Southern Conference and Northern New England were smaller than others. These factors explained somewhat more of the differences in size than they did in survival, accounting for about 12% of the variation.

SUMMARY

Well over ten percent of all the members of the United Church of Christ are members of congregations that did not exist in 1957 or were not part of either of the merging denominations. The new congregations of which they are a part have brought us into contact with different parts of the country and added to our church family people from entirely new ethnic communities. They have completely changed the size and complexion of several conferences, such as Southwest, Florida, Southeast, and both of those in California/Nevada.

The clear majority of our new churches are successful and alive. They include many of the largest churches in the denomination. While the image of new churches is usually an intentional new church start initiated by the denomination, adopted congregations and those initiated by local groups have, not without some problems, added to our rainbow mix. By moving into new settlements and new communities in other parts of the country, we have provided places for individuals and families with long-term roots in our denomination to find vibrant and active places in which to grow in their faith. By being a church of strangers meeting each other, these new congregations are often enabled to be more open to strangers from a wider variety of backgrounds. Often they have opportunities to be creative in worship, education, and even architecture in ways that continuing congregations are not. Their innovations enrich us all.

And we are becoming a more diverse people. In the past, churches of non-European ethnicity were often treated paternalistically. Now engaged with visionary leaders from their own background, African-American, Pacific Islander, Asian and other congregations have moved forth with vitality and energy. We need to continue to empower such indigenous leaders.

We have had good success in founding churches in parts of the country where we are already strong. That should be encouraged and continued. However, since the population of the country is growing most rapidly in places where we are not currently strong, we need a national strategy. Support must be channeled to places of opportunity.

It is good that we have ways of knowing about new starts at their very earliest stages. This way they can be found by United Church people moving to other parts of the country. They can also be welcomed into coalitions of churches with particular interests and receive helpful resources. It is also good that Church in Ministry committees can help Churches in Formation to understand our polity and traditions. However, we need to be careful that we do not stall creative churches in these temporary categories, belabor them with denominational barriers when they are facing other challenges, or allow possibly subconscious ethnic or language prejudices to erect barriers to the movement of God.

In all of this, we need to stand in humility before our wonderful, abundant, life-giving God. Through the grace of God, people we did not know and whose life goals we did not set have come to us to share our common lot. They have brought love and sharing to us from afar. Now we join together on the path that we may all be one. Many of these people come to us from foreign lands where they have been brought up in another culture and spoken another language. Some have experienced tyranny. In these far-off places they have been nurtured by their own Christian communities: churches that have often been poor and struggled against unique difficulties. And yet now, in the Providence of God, they are one with us, a new *oikumene*, a new community. Who is this wonderful God who brings all the peoples of the world together? What shall we learn as we continue to grow with such a God into a new day?

NOTES

1. In these years, 1,013 new churches appeared in the full listings of the *Yearbook*. Even though the United Church of Christ was formed in 1957, no list of United Church of Christ congregations appeared until the 1961 General Synod, in conjunction with the adoption of the Constitution of the Church. Before that separate *Yearbook*[s] were issued for the Evangelical and Reformed Church, and for the General Council of Congregational Christian Churches. Only in voting on the United Church of Christ Constitution did local Congregational Christian Churches decide whether to become part of the merged Church. The Evangelical and Reformed Churches also became part of the merged Church at that time by the majority votes of the Synods of the Church. One hundred ninety-four (194) of the congregations in this study first appeared in reports for 1957 through 1960 (including one Congregational Christian Church listed in 1961). This number includes seventeen (17) congregations that were early joint church starts of Congregational Christian Conferences and Evangelical and Reformed Synods. Six (6) more were proposed churches that were eventually organized as full United Church of Christ congregations after the 1961 Synod. These twenty-three (23) could be considered United Church congregations from their earliest listings. One hundred-fifteen (115) of the one hundred and ninety-four (194) congregations were technically

new Congregational Christian Churches. Five of these opposed the merger and never were formally United Church congregations. They are included here with churches withdrawn. (This is a much smaller percentage of votes against the merger than among other Congregational Christian Churches). Some additional churches in this group initially stayed out of the merger, but later became United Church of Christ. Three of the 115 were closed before the initial votes were taken on joining the United Church. Fifty-six (56) of the one hundred ninety-four (194) congregations were technically new Evangelical and Reformed congregations. Two of these 56 were closed by 1961. The rest of these became United Church congregations through the majority vote of the Synods.

2. Proposed congregations is a category first added to the *Yearbook* for the 1989 volume with data for 1988. It was designed to include both new church starts and other congregations in conversation about joining the Church. In the early days of the United Church, new church starts were listed as full churches when they began worship, even if they were not fully organized. As time went on the strengthening of Church and Ministry procedures began to limit the full lists in the *Yearbooks* to congregations fully accredited by their Associations. The new category was added so that such congregations could receive mailings from denominational agencies, and so that United Church of Christ members who moved to a new town could find these new churches. Over time Conferences have varied their definitions of churches in this category. Many say that the title "proposed" is a misnomer, in that perhaps a majority are truly functioning, worshipping congregations with memberships.

3. Most proposed churches have moved on to full standing. One hundred and twenty-two that have been listed in the *Yearbook* have not moved to full standing. Fifty-nine of these are active proposed churches in the current 2007 *Yearbook.* (There are actually sixty-one churches in the current *Yearbook* list. One is a double list of a Church already in the main *Yearbook* section, and another is an older church re-joining the denomination.) In addition two have merged to other UCC congregations, six had withdrawn or decided not to join the UCC, and 48 are extinct. In addition seven more, while not currently listed in the *Yearbook,* are believed to be living potential UCC congregations.

4. Eight earlier proposed churches were found using Conference publications and ethnic directories. None of these have moved to full standing, one decided not to join the UCC, and seven are considered extinct.

5. Most churches introduced as new churches at the last three Synods have already moved to full or proposed standing in a *Yearbook.* A total of fifty-four (54) have not yet appeared in a *Yearbook.* Twenty-eight of these were introduced for the first time at the 2007 General Synod. They are viable potential UCC congregations. Of the remaining twenty-six, one has merged with another UCC Church, four have withdrawn, or decided not to join the UCC, five are extinct, and sixteen more, first named at either the 2003 or 2005 Synods are viable potential United Church of Christ congregations.

6. Some incorrect double listings of congregations have been eliminated. Some incorrect treatments of existing congregations as if they were new have been eliminated.

7. A total of forty-nine (49) such additional united congregations have been followed.
8. *NOW IS THE TIME FOR NEW CHURCH DEVELOPMENT: A Preliminary Report on 50 Years of Church Development in the United Church of Christ*
9. To identify congregations new to the UCC, the authors reviewed and compared *Yearbook* listings for every year from 1957 to the present for congregations with organizing dates from 1957 onward. They supplemented this information with lists of recent proposed congregations and new churches listed on Synod lists. Some of these congregations were, in fact, mergers of older congregations, with the organization date that of the merged church. Some adoptions used the date they joined the UCC as their organizing date and were included; others used the date the church was originally organized and were excluded if that date was prior to 1957. Their database also contained a few proposed churches not included in this study.
10. *Cambridge Platform,* 1648, XVI, 6, 3.

FIFTY YEARS OF SOCIAL AND ETHICAL PERSPECTIVES AND TEACHINGS

Donald Freeman

Throughout its fifty-year history, the United Church of Christ has been known for its outspoken advocacy and action on the major social and ethical issues with which the USA and the global community have had to grapple. It has often been on the forefront, labeled a "bellwether" in *The New York Times*, raising consciousness and directing attention to matters such as racism and white privilege, peace and militarism, domestic violence, exploitation of children, fair employment practices and discrimination, human rights, genocides, sub-Saharan famine and the AIDS pandemic. This essay reviews briefly a wide array of General Synod statements and actions in their social contexts and then describes more fully the theological and ethical perspectives and teachings which have underlain and informed them. The focus is largely limited to the General Synod because, although each of the seven thousand or so local churches, associations, conferences, instrumentalities, agencies and institutions which make up the UCC—including the General Synod as one—can speak only **for** itself and **to** each other, not **for** each other, the nearest approximation to a church-wide voice in the UCC is the General Synod.

A SURVEY OF ACTIONS

The Call to Christian Action in Society, 1957-1959

Already a half-century before the union to form the UCC, all four of the primary constituent communions which became the UCC had participated in the Federal Council of Churches' proclamation of the *Social Creed of the*

Donald Freeman, now retired, is professor emeritus of Congregational Life at Lancaster Theological Seminary.

Churches. It was the era of the Social Gospel, and the most urgent issues were religion and labor and urbanization: the church's response to the industrial revolution, the treatment of workers, and the growth of cities. The *Creed* advocated several "ideals," including the abolition of child labor, a humane work week, a just wage, protection against occupational hazards, and the right of workers to organize. After their unions in the 1930s the Congregational and Christian Churches conjoined their efforts in a Council for Social Action and the Evangelical and Reformed Church in a Commission on Christian Social Action.

When the Uniting General Synod of the UCC in 1957 moved toward uniting those two social action bodies into one, it was a relatively easy task as mergers go. "Neither agency was incorporated. Neither had invested funds, inhibiting traditions, or a long history. Instead, they were markedly similar in their functions, viewpoints, and programs and it was relatively simple to organize and unite the program." The new agency devoted its work and staff to six areas: Economic Life; International Relations; Race Relations; Religion and Education; Social Welfare; and an Editorial Board for publications. It conducted ten winter and summer institutes in 1957-59, a Washington Seminar, annual European Seminar, two Seminars at the United Nations; consultations on "Churchman [sic!] as Citizen" and "the Church and the Farm Problem," numerous regional seminars, and work on "the church's responsibility for the aging." Most of the energy was invested in educating local church members and calling for local church social action.

The new agency also issued several policy statements in those first two years: on corruption in labor and management; race relations; crisis in education; immigration; US foreign economic policy; freedom, security and atomic weapons; national responsibility and areas of need; anti-union-shop legislation; China policy; Palestinian refugees. Its early attention was especially to civil rights and race relations; but the circumstances of the cold war, including the threat of nuclear holocaust, the Hungarian revolt, and especially the 1958 crisis brewing over China, Taiwan and the islands in the Strait of Formosa shifted priority attention to international relations. This shift was obviated at the Second General Synod in 1959, to which the new agency presented "A Call to Christian Action in Society."[1] In that Call the new agency had listed race relations first; but the Synod changed the order and placed the international issues first. The Synod also officially named the new agency "The Council for Christian Social Action" (CCSA).

In its entirety, that Call proved to be remarkably comprehensive (with a major omission to be noted later) in setting the agenda for the fifty years which have since transpired. Different particulars have evolved, but the basic categories and areas of concern have been rather constant. The churches were called upon to pray, address, and take action in respect of:

I. The World of Nations

- Peace, justice, welfare and the elimination of poverty
- Military (for national security) but not militarization (of foreign policy)
- "an effective and enforceable body of international law" and the United Nations
- Arms reduction, especially nuclear
- Human rights
- Economic and social development
- Christian unity "as a reconciling fellowship among all peoples"

II. American Culture:

- "concentrations of power, controlling the channels of information"
- Disparities of plenty and want
- Public vs. private interests
- Labor and management
- Farmers and farm families; migrant workers and families
- Environment: conservation and development of resources
- Meaningful and just economic institutions and practices
- Elimination of poverty, unemployment, inflation; access to goods and services
- Strengthening the family
- Necessary public services: schools, transportation, health care
- Educational and cultural opportunities for all
- Addictions: alcohol, narcotics, gambling
- Services for special groups of persons—young, aging, handicapped, mentally ill, addicted
- Admission and integration of refugees
- Access to communications, public services, resources
- Treatment and rehabilitation of convicted offenders
- Creative and enriching use of leisure time

III. Race Relations (prefaced by a call to repentance)

- "For the elimination of pride and prejudice from our hearts"

- "For the end of racial segregation and discrimination in our communities—in church life, in housing, in employment, in education, in public accommodations and services, and in the exercise of political rights"
- "For the alleviation of poverty, ignorance, illness, and all other handicaps which are aggravated by unequal opportunity and by segregation imposed by law or custom"
- "For the furtherance of human rights throughout the world and respect for all men [sic!] as persons created in the image of God"

IV. Political Life

(with a preface highlighting the necessity of controversy and compromise)

- For "effective, representative, and responsible government"
- For active participation of Christians in all forms of political life
- "For the critical evaluation, within the fellowship of the church and in the perspective of Christian faith, of the policies and practices of candidates, office holders, and political parties"
- "For a church with bonds of Christian fellowship so strong that it dares to discuss and act upon civic and political issues"
- "For maintaining the independence of the churches and the state, and for creative cooperation between them."

The Call concluded with a Dedication: "To these tasks we dedicate ourselves in the name of God who calls us to seek justice for all [God's] children and to love our neighbor not only in word but in deed. In [God] is our confidence and our trust."

The prefatory paragraphs to the section on American Culture describe eloquently the domestic social context as perceived at the time (and which is remarkably applicable to our time):

> 19. Our cities rise higher. Our suburbs spread afar. Streams of people move from place to place across the land. Astounding inventions provide abundance of goods, swiftness of communication, miracles of healing, and relief from many burdensome tasks. Opportunities for educational and cultural enrichment are multiplied.
>
> 20. In the midst of this abundance, we are beset by much that is trivial, [de!]humanizing, and vulgar. Prodigious plenty tempts us to selfish indulgence while millions of people in our land and abroad live in want. Private consumption has reached unprecedented levels while public services on which all of us depend are starved. Concentrations of power, controlling the channels of information, beguile masses of people into unthinking

conformity and slavish striving for goods that do not satisfy. Much of our leisure time is devoted to forms of entertainment and escape that dull us to the world's need. We are tempted to love things and use people when we should love people and use things. And even in the midst of crowds our lives are often empty, anxious, and alone.

21. Now as always God calls us to a new life that offers genuine meaning, faith, and community. [God] sets before us goals that are higher than comfort and success. [God] summons us to develop our capacities for mental and spiritual growth. [God] frees us from our bondage to the networks of opinion and taste. [God] saves us from calling good evil or evil good. [God] searches the streets of our cities and the by-ways of the countryside—not for the church that takes pride in its popularity, its wealth, or the splendor of its buildings—but for the church that does justice and seeks truth, that cares for people and loves the Gospel, lifting up family, community, and world.

Ensuing Calls, Pronouncements, Proposals for Action, Resolutions, Overtures, and Actions

By the time of General Synod 4 in 1963, the Synod had moved beyond organizational matters to focus more on broader social concerns. It sorted out several different types of agenda, and refined its processes for review and deliberation:

- **Pronouncements**: the most heavyweight theological and ethical statements, subjected to critical evaluation before and during a General Synod, requiring a two-thirds vote, creating a body of practical theology to guide the church over time—next to constitution and by-laws the nearest things to precedent-setting in the UCC

- **Proposals for Action:** based on Pronouncements, calling upon various local churches and church bodies to take specific action in response to specific concerns

- **Resolutions**: declarations of Christian conviction and calls for action, also requiring theological foundation, and committee deliberation, but addressed to more immediate specific issues before a given General Synod, and sometimes calling for the later development of a more full-blown Pronouncement.

- **Overtures,** asking a General Synod to devote some time to discussion and mutual exchange of information and perspectives on a given concern without a proposed outcome—not listed as an option in Standing Rules in the last 25 years but occasionally built into Synod agenda

From then on, General Synods have taken action on two to six Pronouncements and Proposals for Action and what Charles Maxfield has called "a barrage" of resolutions—averaging 33 and as many as 54—relating to social policy.[2] Since 1993, "resolutions of witness" on social issues require a two-thirds vote for adoption, as distinct from other "prudential" resolutions.

A primary center for action on these issues has been maintained in Washington, DC, by the Office for Church in Society and now Justice and Witness Ministries. Much gathering and dissemination of information, as well as lobbying and testifying before Congress and other government agencies, has been carried out in collaboration with a variety of other religious bodies. On a broader scale, for decades the volunteer service program of the UCC has placed committed persons on the scene in church and community agencies both within the USA and worldwide for short and long term service in ministries of compassion and advocacy.

The impact of this history of General Synod actions on the church and on public life in the USA has been manifold and often controversial. Hundreds of instances could be listed. The following are illustrative and are presented under the headings of the Call, but they overlap considerably.

I. THE WORLD OF NATIONS:
Peace, Justice, and a Just Peace Church

1. One of the most dramatic controversial issues in the early years of the UCC was the Vietnam conflict. General Synods 5 and 6 (1965, 1967) called for a negotiated settlement, and by 1969, GS 7 advocated public protest against the war and a policy of withdrawal. Publication of the *Pentagon Papers* led to a more comprehensive plan at GS 8 in 1971, and the bombing of Cambodia increased advocacy for withdrawal. UCC President Robert V. Moss (1969-76) became increasingly outspoken in opposition to the war, and a sizeable portion of delegates to Penn West Conference boycotted a reception for him there in 1974.

2. Conscientious objection, the draft, and amnesty: One of the first resolutions adopted by a General Synod (GS 3, 1961) affirmed the right of conscientious objection and called for educational resources. GS 6 (1967) adopted a carefully-worded pronouncement upholding selective conscientious objection; CCSA established a ministry to educate youth about military and alternative service, and training of draft counselors. GS 7 (1969) adopted a pronouncement on overhaul of the Selective Service System, including a call for a voluntary military; it also issued a statement including "the moral right for reasons of conscience either to enter military service or resist a war and military service" and a call for amnesty for persons "driven into exile" during

the course of the Vietnam war. The next three Synods reiterated and expanded on a policy of unconditional amnesty.

3. United Nations and human rights: In 1961, 1991, and on occasion of the UN 50th anniversary in 1995, General Synods reaffirmed the United Nations, advocated for a World Court and collaboration with a variety of UN agencies and programs. Several resolutions through the years have addressed specific UN emphases (such as the current decade on violence) and areas of human rights violations.

4. Arenas of international conflict: Virtually every General Synod has taken up questions of conflict between nations and peoples. The list has been expansive, including: Israel/Palestine, a most persistent difficult arena; the Soviet Union and international communism; China/Taiwan; Korea; Cuba; Pakistan/India; Portugal and Angola, Mozambique, Guinea Bissau, Namibia, Zimbabwe; The Philippines; Egypt and the Sudan; Biafra/Nigeria; Burundi/Rwanda; Liberia, Niger; Lybia, Algeria; Romania, Hungary, Czechoslovakia, Poland; El Salvador, Guatemala, Nicaragua and Honduras; Iran; Armenia; Afghanistan; Sri Lanka; Germany and reunification; Iraq/Kuwait and the Persian Gulf War; Grenada; Kosovo, Bosnia, Serbia--the Balkan states; Ethiopia, Somalia, Chad, Darfur; and Ireland. The assertions of the General Synods have been pretty consistent throughout these fifty years in respect of all of these arenas:

   - Advocacy for non-combatants and refugees, and for humane US immigration policies
   - Advocacy of human rights, civil rights, and the rights of peoples to self-determination (including, e.g., the rights of Palestinians as well as Israel's right to exist)
   - Support and care for military personnel and their families, but not for militarization as a means of conduct of affairs
   - Truthful and timely communication, not the manipulation of news
   - Multilateral international response, especially through the United Nations; avoidance of unilateral intervention
   - Negotiated cease-fires and settlements involving all affected groups at the table
   - Opposition to first-strike strategies; military intervention always a last resort

- Opposition to profiteering from war and armed conflict
- Use of non-military pressures such as trade embargoes, especially against arms trade, so long as food, medicines and other humanitarian aid can be delivered as needed
- Rebuilding of nations and their economies (analogy: the Marshall Plan)

5. Southern Africa and Apartheid: By 1960 the UCC was voicing concern over human rights violations in South Africa.
   - General Synod 5 (1965) advocated economic sanctions; GS6 extended the area of concern to all of southern Africa, including peoples under Portuguese control.
   - GS7 called for divestment from financial institutions doing business with South Africa.
   - GS8 called for an end to arms sales and for corporate social responsibility.
   - Each subsequent General Synod made these points more emphatically until it came to a head at GS 15 in 1985 with a conflict between rival proposed pronouncements, one on full divestment from all corporations doing business with South Africa, the other, from the Pension Boards, on retention of investments and use of stockholder strategies to effect change in corporate policies and thereby affect the apartheid system. Acting in concert with a number of other denominations, and in solidarity with the South African Council of Churches, the delegates adopted the strategy of full divestment.

   Thankfully, much has changed in southern Africa since 1992.

6. Arms control and nuclear non-proliferation were on the UCC agenda from its beginning. By General Synod 5 in 1965 the emphasis shifted toward disarmament, and several subsequent Synods called for either arms limitation or disarmament. GS 12 (1979) adopted a pronouncement, "Reversing the Arms Race." GS 14 (1983) called for elimination of weapons of mass destruction and denounced first-strike strategies. GS 21 (1997) called for a comprehensive ban on land mines. While generally allowing the need for a military to ensure security and limit violence, the disposition has always been to avoid militarization of foreign policy and international relations.

7. Calls for apology and redress: to Japanese-Americans incarcerated during World War II (GS 13, 1981, and 14, 1983); to the people of Vieques for damages from military occupation and bomb testing (GS 13, 1981);

to the people of Hawaii for complicity in their mistreatment and the overthrow of their government (GS 18, 1991); and to the people of the Marshall islands for damages from nuclear testing (GS 22, 1999). UCC President Paul Sherry conveyed the church's apology personally, and GS 24 (2003) celebrated the US military withdrawal from Vieques.

8. Call for closure of the School of the Americas and the training of persons from Latin America and elsewhere in the use of torture and other unethical tactics (GS 21, 1997), to which has since been added arrests and detentions at Guantanamo Bay and other sites and abuses of the Patriot Act since 2003.

9. General Synod 15 adopted the pronouncement, "Affirming the UCC as a Just Peace Church," in 1985: Justice is a necessary precondition to any lasting peace.[3] Synods and UCC bodies since have struggled to define this position in specific circumstances, somewhere between just war and pacifism, but the general concept has been widely affirmed in the UCC.

10. World poverty and hunger, economic and social development: Paralleling the emphasis on world peace, General Synod 6 (1967) adopted "A Manifesto for American Action in the Struggle Against World Poverty. GS 7 (1969) added family planning; GS 10 (1975) addressed the world food crisis and launched the UCC Hunger Action Program. Causes of hunger were sought, leading to a resolution on global debt at GS 16 in 1987; GS 22 and 23 (1999, 2001) called for support of the Jubilee 2000 effort to erase the debt of 41 nations. The economic as well as social impact of globalization has been an increasing concern, with a pronouncement on transnational business at GS 10 in 1975 and a pronouncement on globalization at GS 24 in 2003. Many UCC churches have been promoting and using Fair Trade coffee, which GS 25 endorsed in 2005.

11. Environment, sustainable life styles and the integrity of creation: General Synod 10 (1975) called for Christian life styles compatible with a sustainable environment. GS 11 and 12 called for renewable sources of energy. GS 14 and 15 (1983, 1985) added toxic waste issues. A UCC report on "Toxic Waste and Race" (GS 16, 1987) has been hailed as a landmark study, with an update coming out in 2007.

    - GS 16 (1987) was brazen enough to change the order of the World Council of Churches priorities, placing Integrity of Creation ahead of Justice and Peace.

- The UCC has sent delegates to the earth summits beginning in 1991, and advocated observance of the Kyoto protocols.
- Global warming (climate change) was addressed by GS 22 (1999).
- In 2006 the TV documentary, "Troubled Waters," was produced by the UCC, narrated by UCC member Lynn Redgrave, and aired on 115 ABC stations. Access to potable water, especially by persons in poverty, is threatened by both pollution and the privatization of water supplies, and may become the 21st century's greatest crisis.

The remaining three divisions of the Call to Christian Action in Society all focused on the USA: American Culture, Race Relations, and Political Life

II. AMERICAN CULTURE

1. The first item in the Call concerned "concentrations of power, controlling the channels of information," and brought the church's attention to the media:

    - In 1959, Everett Parker and the UCC Office of Communication (OC) challenged discriminatory rules of the Federal Communications Commission in court and, by 1964, won access to the media by minority groups. OC also gained FCC regulations prohibiting telephone conglomerates from denying telephone access to low-income neighborhoods. It has taken continued vigilance and repeated effort to maintain these victories.
    - GS 9 in 1973 called for enforcement of the FCC fairness doctrine and the right of people to know.
    - GS 11 (1977) adopted a pronouncement on the exploitation of gratuitous violence and sex in the media. GS 16 (1987) addressed pornography, with a special concern for children, and GS 20 (1995) focused again on violence in the media.
    - GS 12 in 1979 advocated for third world access to modern communication technology.
    - The UCC Office of Communication has been a major participant in the Media Empowerment Project, which works to hold local media accountable to the needs of diverse communities. For instance, in 2005 Texas passed a law enabling media companies to skirt an FCC requirement, and TimeWarner terminated local access Channel 20

in San Antonio; local MEP action persuaded the city to require its reinstatement in 2006.

- In 2005 the OC filed suit against Univision for using non-educational programs to fulfil federal requirements to provide educational programs for children. The courts agreed, and Univision was fined $24 million in 2007.

2. The "disparities of plenty and want" have worsened in these fifty years. Poverty is intertwined with racism, sexism and classism. General Synod actions have included:

   - An early pronouncement (GS 4, 1963) calling for federal legislation to ensure equality of opportunity and fair employment practices for all citizens, followed by advocacy for affirmative action within the church as well as society, support for the War on Poverty, and advocacy for employee rights
   - **Housing:** GS 4 also addressed urbanization, with housing as a major issue. GS 5 condemned unfair housing practices, GS 6 related housing to school desegregation, and GS 7 (1969) called for development of affordable housing for lower income persons, especially elderly
   - **Empowerment:** GS 6 (1967) advocated, above all, "Solution of the Problems of the Poor by the Poor"
   - **Health care:** GS 6 (1967) also sought allegiance with medical professionals in declaring health care to be a basic human right; GS 8, 9, and 10 advocated increasingly comprehensive health care reform, including universal health insurance. This was capped by a pronouncement by GS 18 (1991), "Toward an Accessible Universal Health Care System." The "twin scandals" of poverty and access to health care were highlighted at GS 23 in 2001 and are being addressed by Justice and Witness Ministries.
   - **Tax equity:** beginning with the pronouncement by GS 7 in 1969, "Sharing the Cost of Government Fairly," followed by church-wide education on tax justice in the 70s, and frequent protests into the 21st century against regressive tax "reforms."
   - **Social services:** Advocating federal budget priorities to ensure adequate funding of social services, especially as they relate to children (GS 9, 1973 and most synods since). GS 21 (1997) condemned the 1996 Federal Welfare Reform Act as unconscionable, and subsequent synods have hailed the benefits and pointed out the damages from the repeated "reforms" of the welfare system, especially to children in poverty.

- In 1983, UCC leaders and members were highly visible in the March for Jobs and Freedom, commemorating the 20th anniversary of the 1963 March on Washington. A similar march took place around the 40th anniversary in 2003.

3. Farmers, migrant workers, and their families:

- Both small farmers and migrant workers were lifted up in the Call in 1959.
- GS 3 (1961) addressed issues of wages, housing, child care, education and public services to migrant workers.
- In 1971, with major leadership from the United Church Board for Homeland Ministries, the interfaith National Farm Worker Ministry was launched.
- In a dramatic act of solidarity funded by the Board for Homeland Ministries, General Synod 9 (1973), while meeting in St. Louis, sent a delegation of 92 persons to join the United Farm Workers' strike in the lettuce fields of the Coachella valley in California. A boycott of non-union lettuce was begun, and GS 12 in 1979 added Chiquita bananas to the boycott. GS 15 (1985) called for a boycott of non-union table grapes. Subsequent boycotts challenged Campbell's soup, Nor Pac, and Mount Olive Pickles. GS 23 (2001) voted to boycott Taco Bell tomatoes in support of the Immokalee Indians, and a successful outcome was celebrated at GS 25 in 2005.
- GS 11 (1977) called for a pronouncement on the quality of life in rural America, which was adopted by GS 12. GS 14, 15 and 16 addressed a growing farm crisis throughout the 1980s, worsened by public economic policies and private loaning practices.

4. Services for special groups of persons:

- Children and youth, aging, mental illness, addictions, refugees, incarcerated persons,—all were concerns of General Synods over the years.
- The UCC has been a major participant in the Inter-religious Coalition on Smoking and Health and in the Campaign for Tobacco-free Kids.
- The Board for Homeland Ministries provided grants and loans to local churches to make their facilities accessible to all.
- A dramatic event was the Americans with Disabilities Act in 1990: A long time coming. Harold Wilke of UCC Persons with Disabilities was a prime mover and received the first pen at the signing from President George H. W. Bush, accepting it with his toes. A2A ("ac-

cessible to all") has become one of the key attributes of the UCC's "extravagant welcome" in the 21st century.

III. Racial Justice and a Multi-Racial, Multi-Cultural Church

Although almost overwhelmingly Euro-American and White, the United Church of Christ began with a small constituency of people of color--from the historic work of the American Missionary Association and missionaries worldwide among black, native American and immigrant peoples. The new denomination hailed the Civil Rights Act of 1957, and the Call to Christian Action in Society of 1959 placed a high priority on racial concerns. The next five Synods addressed racial justice as a central crisis of the nation—in church as well as society--with focus on civil rights, education, employment and just compensation. Among the efforts to establish racial justice and overcome racism have been the following:

- Continuation of the American Missionary Association's annual Institute of Race Relations at Fisk University; moreover, beginning in 1961 the Board for Homeland Ministries provided facilities for the Citizen Education Project, staffed by Andrew Young, which trained over 1,000 literacy teachers and leaders of the civil rights movement in collaboration with the Southern Christian Leadership Conference
- Participation in the 1963 March on Washington for Jobs and Freedom with Martin Luther King, Jr., and other subsequent marches
- Establishment of the Committee on Racial Justice Now at General Synod 4 in 1963
- Advocacy for the Civil Rights Act (1964) and Voting Rights Act (1965); voter education and registration were pursued especially throughout the 1960s
- GS 7 (1969) struggled with the Black Manifesto and responded in part to its demands. The Committee on Racial Justice Now was elevated to the Commission for Racial Justice (CRJ)
- Support for the Wilmington 10 (one of whom was CRJ field worker Benjamin Chavis) from their arrest in 1971 on the charge of firebombing a grocery store through their conviction and finally acquittal in 1980

Several other social and economic issues were discerned to have racism at their cores, with action taken accordingly, including migrant farm workers (1973), immigration (pronouncement, 1981), toxic waste dumps (1981, 1983, major report in 1987), and AIDS (1983, pronouncement 1987).

Several minority caucuses developed in the church and were increasingly empowered:

- 1967, Racial Justice Now gathered Ministers for Racial and Social Justice (MRSJ). United Black Christians (UBC) arose as an avenue for lay participation.
- 1971, General Synod 8 reaffirmed racial concerns as a priority, and created the Council for American Indian Ministries (CAIM)
- 1973, caucus leading to the Council for Pacific and Asian-American Ministries (PAAM) in 1975
- 1975, caucus leading to the Council for Hispanic Ministries (CHM) in 1977
- 1979, GS 12 added funding for these bodies to the Budget of the General Synod
- 1983, GS 14 created the Council for Racial and Ethnic Ministries (COREM) as a table for all of these groups
- GS 16 (1987) made a strong statement against racism and called for a more comprehensive message. Hispanic persons, believing they were ignored, walked out of that Synod, adding further urgency to the issue.
- *Pastoral Letter on Contemporary Racism and the Role of the Church* was issued jointly by 54 national officers and conference ministers of the UCC in 1991, the only "encyclical" of its kind to date, with a study and action guide for local church use.
- Subsequently, a bylaw amendment gave the Executive Council authority to add representatives of "underrepresented constituencies" to its membership. (Several instrumentalities had already intentionally included minority members on their boards.) 1997 and 1999 revisions of the Constitution and Bylaws gave the COREM bodies seats on the Executive Council and directorates of the covenanted ministries, effective in 2000.

The UCC has taken on the hopeful identity and ongoing task of becoming a multi-racial and multi-cultural church. This is especially evident in the composition of the staff in the national settings of the church.

IV. Political life

- The Call in 1959 included "effective, representative, and responsible government." General Synods over the years have been faithful critics. The latest such resolution was "A Call for Truth-telling and

Standards of Ethics in Public Life," by GS 25 in 2005.

- For decades the UCC Office for Church in Society and now Justice and Witness Ministries has maintained an office in Washington DC, testifying before legislative, executive and judicial bodies, hosting and educating delegations from local churches in lobbying their elected representatives, and providing a steady stream of information via print and electronic media. Much of this work is done on an ecumenical basis.
- The OCIS and now JWM have provided wise counsel to the church on observing the boundary between lawful and illegitimate advocacy and lobbying. The church has not, for instance, supported any candidate for elected office; but it has spoken out on policies and appointments, including the controversial nomination of Robert Bork to the Supreme Court which was opposed (with significant disagreement and abstention) by GS 18 in 1991.

Overlooked until later: Emergent issues related to human sexuality

The Call to Christian Action in Society reveals the church's lack of consciousness about several areas of concern which emerged (also with much controversy) during the ensuing fifty years, especially with the development of the feminist movement. They all fall under the umbrella of human sexuality and were hardly a matter of leaders' awareness in 1957:

1. Women in church and society:
    - This area of concern was on CCSA's radar screen in 1963, but it was not until 1969 that a General Synod (GS 7) first took formal action, affirming the principle of equality of the sexes.
    - CCSA advocated reproductive choice and sex education in 1970.
    - In 1971 General Synod 8 mobilized the UCC to address women's concerns more comprehensively, including inclusive language, discrimination in employment and compensation, and Roe v. Wade.
    - GS 9 (1973) created the Task Force on Women in Church and Society and called for nine specific actions to eliminate sex and race discrimination. The Task Force was made the Coordinating Center for Women in 1979 (GS 12), became an established instrumentality in 1987 (GS 16), and was incorporated into Justice and Witness Ministries with the restructure of 1999-2001.
    - GS 10 through 14 (1975-83) advocated ratification of the Equal Rights Amendment.

- GS 13 and 14 focused on violence against women; the UCC joined the UN convention against discrimination of women throughout the 1980s, and GS 21 (1997) called for an end to female genital mutilation.

2. Sexual minorities:

- In 1969, CCSA was urging honest discussion throughout the church and opposing discrimination in employment, the criminalization of consensual homosexual expression, and entrapment practices in law enforcement. The UCC Executive Council advocated sex education in homes, schools and churches, especially as a response to pornography.

- After the ordination of William Johnson, an openly gay man, in 1972, the Executive Council directed the development of resources related to ordination and recommended that homosexuality per se not be a bar to ordination.

- General Synod 10 in 1975 adopted a pronouncement on civil liberties without discrimination related to affectional sexual preference and commissioned a comprehensive study of human sexuality. *Human Sexuality: A Preliminary Study* occupied much of General Synod 11 in 1977, leading a substantial minority of over 25 percent to launch United Church People for Biblical Witness (later renamed Biblical Witness Fellowship).

- GS 15 (1985) called on local churches to covenant as *open and affirming* of lesbian, gay, bisexual and transgendered persons, and GS 23 (2001) welcomed and celebrated their gifts for ministry, including ordained ministry.

- GS 21 (1997) upheld fidelity "in marriage and in other covenanted relationships."

- Perhaps the most divisive action in recent years was the adoption of a resolution "In Support of Equal Marriage Rights for All" by GS 25 in 2005, defining marriage without reference to gender affirmed a more inclusive definition of marriage. It passed the Synod by well more than the required two-thirds, but more than a hundred local churches have disaffiliated from the UCC as a consequence, and a number of churches, often self-labeled ECOT (evangelical, conservative, orthodox, or traditional) have created a "constructive dissent" group called Faithful and Welcoming Churches (FWC).[4] It should be noted, on the other hand, that some churches have become UCC in response to the UCC's open and affirming stance.

- By the beginning of 2007, 710 local churches (about twelve percent) and 14 conferences have declared themselves open and affirming.

3. Abortion and reproductive choice:

As noted above, in 1970 CCSA placed its advocacy of reproductive choice in a package with advocacy of sex education and family planning. General Synod 8 adopted this in 1971 and hailed Roe v. Wade. Succeeding Synods have reaffirmed these again and again, along with advocacy of contraception to reduce or eliminate unchosen pregnancies, and the rights of women generally.

4. Inclusive language:

General Synod 9 included this in its reaffirmation of the mandate to the Task Force on Women in Church and Society in 1973, and GS 11 (1977) called for inclusive language in preparation of a new Book of Worship. Inclusive language guidelines were developed and became normative in the national setting of the UCC, and GS 17 (1989) called for their refinement and application especially in respect of biblical texts and translations. There has been significant objection to inclusive language revisions, especially with the reception of *The New Century Hymnal* (1993).

5. Violence, sexual harassment and abuse:

General Synods 13 and 14 addressed violence in relation to women, children and youth in 1981 and 1983. The Executive Council took strong policy action on sexual harassment in the UCC in 1982; GS 17 called in 1989 for a pronouncement on sexual harassment, which was adopted by GS 18 in 1991; and GS 20 addressed violence in the media again in 1995.

6. AIDS:

General Synod 14 (1983) called for expansion of compassionate programs and research. GS 16 (1987) adopted a major pronouncement on "the pandemic," and AIDS education materials and programs were developed, the most recent of which is a curriculum, *Affirming Persons, Saving Lives*, by Justice and Witness Ministries (United Church Press, 2004). Wider Church Ministries continues to be deeply involved in AIDS ministries in Africa and worldwide.

7. Comprehensive sex education:

From 1971 the UCC has advocated and produced materials for sex education. More recently, *Our Whole Lives—Sexuality and Our Faith* and *Created in*

God's Image: A Human Sexuality Education Program for Ministry and Mission, a comprehensive educational series for children and adults with teacher training components, were produced in collaboration with the Unitarian Universalist Association.

THEOLOGICAL FOUNDATIONS FOR SOCIAL ACTION:

Authoritative Resources and Teaching

The United Church of Christ has a rich and diverse theological heritage: According to the Preamble to its *Constitution,* it looks to and claims as its own the scriptures, the ancient creeds, the insights of the Reformers, and the continuing inspiration and guidance of the Holy Spirit in every generation. Its roots were Euro-American, primarily "Reformed" in the generic sense of that term, shaped by both pietism and the Enlightenment as well as the pre-Reformation church and the Renaissance.

The (German) Reformed Church in the US was Calvinistic with some Lutheran influence, and its Mercersburg movement embraced the whole of Christian tradition, including medieval Catholicism. Congregationalism was Calvinistic out of an Anglican context. Both of these communions had participated in the two Great Awakenings in various ways, as contributors and as resistors. The Christian churches came from Methodist, Baptist and Presbyterian backgrounds and participated in the second Great Awakening. The Evangelical Synod was a Lutheran/Reformed union with pietism as a formative influence. All four traditions had an ecumenical vision and vocation: to realize the church as the one body of Christ. And all four shared a Calvinistic conviction of the sovereignty of God over all of human life, social, political and economic as well as personal, spiritual and moral.

To these four primary traditions must be added a variety of groups and persons with African, Asian, east European, Latin American and Pacific Island roots, and movements such as feminism and gay rights, each adding their voice and expanding the social consciousness of the church as a whole.

That conviction—that God is sovereign, or that Christ is Lord and Master (now usually avoiding the language of domination)—has been and remains the foundation of the social and ethical teaching and activism of the United Church of Christ. But how is the church to discern and articulate the will and the way of God in respect of the particular, ever-changing circumstances of day-to-day life?

An examination of the pronouncements, proposals for action, resolutions of witness, and educational materials generated by the UCC over these first fifty years finds them virtually always grounded in the four authoritative sources sometimes called the Wesleyan quadrilateral: scripture, tradition, experience, and reason. To these, or within these, John Macquarrie has added culture as a major source and points to claims of revelation involved.[5] Each of these bears examination in terms of how they have functioned in the United Church of Christ. It should be noted, however, that the UCC has often been said to give more attention to the social action it advocates than to the grounds upon which such action is based.

A. Scripture

Most folk in the UCC have always turned to scripture as preeminent authority for discerning the will and way of God, but often been in conflict over how scripture is to be used in the process. A committee hearing on sexuality resolutions at General Synod 14 (Pittsburgh, 1983) vividly revealed four different--but not mutually exclusive and often overlapping--ways of drawing upon the scriptures. These ways might be identified in shorthand as prescriptive, descriptive, characterological, and relational:

1. *Prescriptive:* The first volley in the interchange was launched by persons who used the Bible prescriptively as a collection of "truths"--precepts and rules quoted by chapter and verse, some would say without human interpretation (although critics claimed that, at the least, human selectivity was involved). Revelation is found in propositional form.

2. *Descriptive:* The second volley came from a different quarter, lifting up what they thought of as "the weightier matters" of the Bible: justice, mercy, truth, peace. Throughout the 1970s and 1980s these were held together in UCC publications under the Hebrew vision of *shalom* (*eiréne* in the New Testament), which includes personal, social, and even environmental well-being as well as, as commonly translated, peace. Proponents sometimes cited passages, especially from the prophets, as prescriptively as those who launched the first volley, but the approach to scripture was generally more deliberative: What is the Biblical vision of shalom, and how can it be realized "on earth as it is in heaven"?

3. *Characterological:* These two points of view were heavily rationalistic, each in its own way and each with its own kind of piety. It wasn't long before a third, more classically pietistic approach was introduced into the discussion: What is in the character and spirit of Jesus the Christ? (More simply, What would Jesus do?) Scripture illumines for us the heart and mind of God incarnate and calls and forms us to have this same heart and mind among ourselves. The focus is not on the letter so much as the spirit.

4. *Relational:* A fourth use of scripture, also focused more on the spirit discerned through the letter, emerged more gradually: The scriptures describe the nature and behavior of God's people not just as individuals but as a community. Through our engagement together with the Biblical text, the Holy Spirit exercises a formative influence on our corporate life: how we interact with one another, with all other people, and with all of creation. The primary community thus formed, albeit imperfectly, is the church itself. The very ability of the Synod delegates to deal with such controversial issues as the ones in that hearing bears testimony to this formative influence.

It must be said that, at that General Synod and probably across the UCC as a whole throughout its history, the four approaches to scripture have not borne equal weight. Bearing in mind again that they are not mutually exclusive, it may be estimated that the deliberative approach has predominated, followed by the characterological; the communal/relational is more tacit, and not as often explicitly asserted; the prescriptive approach has generally been vocal, whether citing legalistic precepts (in the minority) or (more often) prophetic proclamations. In fact, many of the resolutions in the middle of the fifty-year span drew upon scripture only briefly, leaving the appearance of a church which was reluctant to cite scripture lest it be accused of proof-texting or literalism. The question was sometimes raised, Where's the Bible?

B. Tradition

Tradition is so multi-faceted in the United Church of Christ that summarizing its influence (recognizing our heritage, really a plural: "their influence") on social and ethical teaching and action is a daunting task. To start with, all understandings of scripture are shaped by traditions regarding both content and method, and the four uses of scripture reviewed above are, after all, traditions in their own right.

The UCC has always been immersed in the wider U.S. and world Christian conversations about ethics, politics, economics and social life. In 1957 neo-orthodoxy was rivaling if not overshadowing the previous generations of liberalism and stimulating a variety of neo-liberal perspectives. The great elder ethicists of the UCC and of American Protestantism included the Niebuhr brothers out of the Evangelical Synod—H. Richard having major influence on ethical theory, Reinhold having greater influence in socio-political arenas, secular as well as religious. The two brothers had had a famous difference of opinion about the Sino-Japanese War twenty years before: Reinhold, who resigned from the more pacifistic Fellowship of Reconciliation, urged political realism and the need to act with force to affect the balance of power against fascism, while Richard, trusting more in the influence of the divine in history, advocated "The Grace of Doing Nothing." Their somewhat differing emphases shaped a whole generation of younger theologian-ethicists: Dietrich Bonhoeffer's life and writings were of major influence, as well as other German theologians such as Karl Barth, Emil Brunner, Rudolf Bultmann, Helmut Thielicke, and, some years later, Jürgen Moltmann. By the 1970s, various forms of liberation theology were in the ascendancy, including African-American, Latin, Asian, feminist and then womanist voices. All of these voices wielded significant influence on UCC advocacy and action, as can be discerned in the list of actions in section I above.

The UCC immediately began to generate its own traditions. The Call to Christian Social Action of 1959 has been previously described, along with its continuing influence into this 21st century. Perhaps even more influential has been another and more remarkable document from that same year, the UCC *Statement of Faith*.

As the *Statement* was recited at Oberlin that year, it was the verbs which stood out, most of them in present or unceasing tense: It sang—sang of the mighty acts of God, consonant with both the neo-orthodoxy and neo-liberalism—and the existentialism--of the day, but also consonant with the whole historic Christian story. Although evidently trinitarian in spirit, it did not repeat the historic issues about the nature of God: God's nature is revealed by God's deeds, in creation and call, in covenant and promise, in the work of the Holy Spirit, and centrally "in Jesus Christ, the man of Nazareth." It gave shape to a tradition in the image of God: a church of deeds. A few phrases and sentences from the Statement of Faith have powerfully shaped the UCC and have been cited over and over again in pronouncements, resolutions, actions, and publications:

- God "seeks in holy love to save **all** people from aimlessness and sin." The Synod insisted on the adjective, "all." Little was it then foreseen how inclusive this theologically-driven church was to strive to become: M&M (multiracial and multicultural), O&A (open and affirming of various sexual orientations), A2A (accessible to all of differing abilities)—a church of extravagant welcome, with baptism and holy communion (and occasionally footwashing) celebrated as God's inclusive acts.

- "In Jesus Christ, the man of Nazareth, [God] has come to us and **shared our common lot** . . .." The solidarity of God with ordinary humans, especially "the least of these," is consonant with the inclusion of all people, and the UCC Coordinating Center for Women took from this phrase the title of its major periodical, *Common Lot*.

- "... reconciling the world to [God's]self." The church's ministry is not of condemnation but of reconciliation, breaking down walls of hostility and overcoming evil with good.
- "... to accept the cost and joy of discipleship ...

  "to be [God's] servants in the service of [the whole human family] ...

  "and resist the powers of evil

  "courage in the struggle for justice and peace,

  "[God's] presence in trial and rejoicing ..."

  "Courage in the Struggle" became the title of the primary periodical of the UCC Office for Church in Society, since 2000 the Covenanted Justice and Peace Ministry. There is an enduring wisdom in the recognition of "cost," "resist," "struggle" and "trial"; and power in the affirmations of "presence," "courage" and "rejoicing."
- And it should be noted that there is considerable consonance between the unceasing-present verbs of 1959 (calls, creates, sets, seeks, judges, promises, along with conquering, reconciling, bestowing, renewing, binding) and the 21st century UCC assertion that "God is still speaking," and that the most recent punctuation mark celebrated for the word of God is a comma and not a period.

An even more fundamental tradition-setter is the Preamble to the *Constitution* of the UCC, adopted at the recessed General Synod 2 session of 1960: That Jesus Christ is "sole head of the church" makes all human authority in the church—and, by extension, in the world—relative, limited, and more level. Leadership is not by "lording over" but by servanthood, exercising power not to dominate but to empower. Although there have been instances of both top-down power and unnecessarily weak leadership in the history of the UCC, its polity has generally remained participatory—sometimes to a fault. And its advocacy and action in social, political and economic arenas has supported servant leadership.

It is unfortunate that the title, "Lord," is so burdened with a history of domination. Biblically, in Philippians 2.11 it is a powerful affirmation of Jesus as God's Christ, implicitly bestowing on Jesus the very name of God (YHWH->*adonai*->*kyrios*=Lord). Politically, it placed all human lords under the sole Lordship of this one who exercised authority not by lording over but by serving. General Synod 11 in 1977 called for a book of worship in inclusive language which avoids the language of domination, therefore generally avoids Lord, and virtually all UCC publications since, including the *New Century Hymnal*, have attempted to do so.

C. Experience

The God who is still speaking is first a God who is still listening. The Biblical God ***hears***: hears the groans of creation; the cry of blood from the ground; the cry of anguish from the oppressed, the ostracized, the barren, and the abandoned; intentional and unintentional prayers; the noise of children, and even the stones which cry out when the human voices are silenced. UCC theologies, social and ethical teachings have therefore typically paid much heed to human experience. Great lengths have been taken, often at considerable expense, to insure that the tables where deliberations take place and decisions are made have included and taken account of the voices of the various persons and groups who may have a stake in or be affected by the outcomes. General Synod plenary agenda, committee hearings, and Executive Council minutes reveal a stream of such persons as resource persons and collaborators, and the inclusion of "underrepresented constituencies" was built into revised By-laws.

This has been at considerable risk: Time and again the UCC (meaning the national setting, including General Synod) has been characterized as "at the mercy of special interests," or "politically [in presumed contrast to theologically] correct," especially by some of its disgruntled members. (And typically the accusers have not seen the special interests in their own eyes.) Time and again Synod delegates have been "swayed"—by emotions? by the Holy Spirit? at any rate, had their minds changed—by the testimonies of affected persons. One Conference's delegation to General Synod 10 (1975) voted almost unanimously against the resolution supportive of civil rights without regard to sexual orientation; its delegation to the next Synod (11, 1977), after personal encounters with gay delegates, lengthy debate and tearful caucuses over the sexuality study, voted over half in favor, and then anguished over how to interpret their votes back home.

Experience includes not only personal interaction, physical sensation and observation, but also internal phenomena. Spiritual disciplines such as meditation and contemplation are experiential in nature and often engage scripture, liturgies, sacraments, and the voice of conscience. The dispute over what kind of hearing to give to voices of experience has been, it would appear, analogous to the traditional tension between pietism and rationalism—pietism taking regard of human experience, rationalism suspicious of the corruptive potential of emotions. Rationalism despises "crimes of passion" while pietism despises "crimes of logic." The UCC is an heir to and home of both traditions.

Experience and tradition are further interrelated: There is no experience apart from its organization and interpretation by the person(s) involved, and various aspects of tradition inform that organizing and interpreting. In fact, it can be said that tradition is largely a preservation of the experience of prior generations.[6] The UCC has tended to give considerable weight to the experience of contemporaries and therefore to revise and reshape theological understandings which come out of traditions, even as the descriptions of new experience have been shaped by various traditions.

D. Reason— including imagination and other forms of mental activity

Classical dogmatic theology often derived its ensuing ethics, economics, and politics by deduction from given dogmatic premises. Deductive reasoning, logic, was presumed to be an infallible means to truth—provided that the premises from which it began were true. But experience provides anecdotes and patterns, hopes and fears, dreams and visions rather than axioms, and when ethics, etc., take various experiences into consideration, reason often arrives (more often inductively) at a corresponding variety of conclusions. Reason is an invaluable tool, and critique is one of the greatest exercises of reason. Virtually every UCC pronouncement, etc., is well reasoned, but so are the counter-arguments. As Epictetus said in ancient Greece, reason may be unable to produce fruit but it is indispensable for weighing and measuring. Reason is not immune to shaping by tradition. In fact, there is a variety of traditions in the exercise of reason, including the uses of reason to interpret scripture, creeds, and other historical texts. The ways we think are culturally conditioned.

Dreams and visions are products of reasoning in a more imaginative mode; and theology, in the last two centuries at least, has been shaped by Romanticism, which embraced and sometimes exalted imagination, as much as Rationalism, which held imagination more suspect as a source of error. In fact, imagination has sometimes been lifted up as a channel of revelation, as one finds in the tradition from Coleridge to theologians Austin Farrer and Ray L. Hart.[7] Dreams and visions have often been inspired and informed by scripture, tradition, and experience, including the spiritual practices of meditation and contemplation. Visions are often rooted in the past, but look more toward the future.

Shalom is such a vision, and the history of UCC pronouncements, resolutions and actions evidences the repeated formative influence of various visions of *shalom*. The sacraments are often experienced as dramatic enactments of visions such as the gathering of God's people and the heavenly banquet, and UCC pronouncements and actions have often grown out of and been supported by sacramental theology. Visions of this sort bring together all of the classical authorities, scripture, tradition, experience, and reason, and this consonance of authorities adds to their power.

Visions can also be misleading. Conflicts over pronouncements, resolutions and actions have often been and will continue to be the consequence of variances in dreams and dreads. Ideologies generally envision human existence as the ideologues hope (or fear) it will come to be, and ideologies may be constructive or destructive, powerful sources of good or evil or a mixture of both. Some negative visions are useful as guides for what to avoid or overcome. The challenge to the UCC, as to all religious communities, is to discern the spirits—to discern which visions are intimations of the way and will of God, inspired by the Holy Spirit, consonant with the mind and heart of Christ.

E. Culture

The influence of culture ("the world") on social and ethical pronouncements and actions has often been viewed negatively, and rightly so; but culture itself can be a positive as well as negative source or resource. In fact, God is portrayed in the scriptures as sovereign of the universe, capable of working through pagan and secular as well as religious means, and various cultures have exhibited values derived from religious traditions. Culture and faith have often shaped one another; and whereas culture may have corrupted or perverted the values it has drawn from religion, it may sometimes be argued that culture has been more faithful in upholding some values than the religions from which they came.

Culture has often been allied with reason, and experience generally bears the imprint of the cultural context. But traditions—specifically the church's traditions—also bear the imprint of the cultures in which they developed and with which they have been preserved and in some ways perverted. This is true of scripture itself, in that the very languages and worldviews of the peoples to whom the scriptures were first addressed both carried and shaped (sometimes mis-shaped) the story of God's deeds and relations with peoples and creation. John Calvin and much of Reformed tradition have embraced a theology of accommodation: that scripture itself reveals how much God accommodates God's word to the ability of the people to understand or at least get the drift of it. There is no such thing as a culture-free reading of scripture, recital of tradition, description of experience, or exercise of reason.

The critique of UCC resolutions and actions has often been that they reflect values of "the world" more than the gospel; that, as mentioned above, they are "politically correct" rather than theologically sound; or that they are the work of "special interest groups." But often it is difficult to discern which side of an argument is more faithful, which is more worldly, and which is more beholden to special interests. Some have argued, for instance, that the General Synods' affirmations of homosexuality are a worldly perversion of the gospel, while others have argued, on the other side, that the anti-homosexuality of the critics reveals the triumph of cultural bias over the gospel. Each side believes itself to be passionately embracing the gospel.

General Synods have adopted most of their pronouncements, proposals for action, and resolutions of witness--and defeated others--by heavy pluralities: they require two-thirds, and when the plurality is not at least 75 percent the minority has the right to affix its contrary report to the adopted text. In my memory at least, a report from a minority of at least 25 percent happened only once, over the sexuality study at General Synod 11 (1977). Though there have often been highly vocal advocates at the opposite poles on an issue, the committee and plenary hearings and deliberations have generally revealed a large body closer to the center than the extremes—definitively tilted toward one side or the other but not without varying measures of hesitation, uncertainty, and respect and appreciation of the variety of convictions and points of view expressed. The UCC is not uncomfortable with and not paralyzed by "the entertainment of doubt."[8] Persons who find doubt distressing may also be distressed with the UCC.

The above survey of UCC actions and their grounds would be incomplete without citing a major source of contributions to the literature of religion and society: The historic Pilgrim Press has produced a steady stream of books for the general trade, and the United Church Press an equally steady stream of print resources especially for the church—many of these publications on the cutting edge of the controversial social issues of the last half-century and the present new century.

THE STILL-SPEAKING INITIATIVE AND A CHURCH OF EXTRAVAGANT WELCOME

Inclusiveness was an attribute of God already tacitly recognized in the *Statement of Faith* in 1959, and over the UCC's 50-year history the implications of this attribute of God have become more radically evident, as Synod after Synod explicitly named and embraced groups of people who have been marginalized or excluded, intentionally or by default, from the center of the church's life as well as from the world's societies. It was not long before diversity was acknowledged and celebrated as a correlative to inclusiveness. Theologically, they are entailed by the sacraments of baptism and holy communion and by a holy spirit which knows no human bounds.

After four years of discussion, General Synod 19 in 1993 adopted *Toward the Twenty-first Century: A Statement of Commitment*: to be and become "A Church Inclusive of All People" as well as "attentive to the Word," "responsive to God's call," and "supportive of one another." The themes of the first three General Synods in the 21st century reiterated this commitment:

- 2001, GS 23, "Gather at the Welcome Table," jointly with the Christian Church (Disciples of Christ)
- 2003, GS 24, "God is Still Speaking"
- 2005, GS 25, "Come Listen, Go Serve: God is Still Speaking"

The Still Speaking Initiative has been dramatic and powerful. It is rooted in pastor John Robinson's address to the departing Mayflower pilgrims in 1619, "God has yet more light to break forth from [God's] holy word," and was launched with the citation of a line from Gracie Allen, "Never put a period where God has placed a comma."

The Initiative also marks the UCC's biggest venture into the world of television advertising. A spot was produced for TV, featuring two "bouncers" in front of a church door letting some people in while turning away others, and concluding with a statement about the UCC, "Jesus didn't turn people away, and neither do we." It was designed for both major network and cable broadcast in Advent of 2004 and financed through a special fund drive throughout the church. In a block which turned out to be fortuitous, NBC and CBS refused to show it, saying that it was "too controversial." Other media picked up on their refusal as newsworthy and gave the UCC far more exposure and attention than might otherwise have been the case. The result has been hundreds of thousands of "hits" on the UCC web page, including many persons with negative past church experience looking for a new church home.

GS 25 (2005) was an occasion to review the video and celebrate the initiative, complete with the two bouncers and Spongebob Squarepants. A second spot is scheduled for showing during Lent of 2007.

The proclamation of a still-speaking God has confirmed the evolving identity of the UCC as an inclusive, multi-racial, multi-cultural church, open and affirming, accessible to all. The comma has become another logo for the UCC, and "God is Still Speaking" has become the UCC's brand in the marketplace of contemporary religion.

DISPARITY BETWEEN NATIONAL AND LOCAL SETTINGS OF THE UCC

The United Church of Christ is a conglomeration of nearly 7,000 semi-autonomous bodies—local churches, associations, conferences, general synods, national covenanted ministries, seminaries, colleges and a variety of institutions and agencies—bound together by a confession of faith that Jesus Christ is son of God, savior, and sole head of the church, and by a uniquely covenantal polity. The *Constitution* of the United Church of Christ recognizes that each body is responsible for itself, and authorizes no body, not even the General Synod, to speak **for** all of these; each body may speak **to** the others and is covenanted to take seriously what each of the others has to say, but not necessarily to agree. As a consequence, dissent is not uncommon. Unfortunately, inattentiveness and indifference are at least as common.

The so-called gap between local church members and General Synods is largely a gap between members and members, in that the first qualification of every delegate to vote at GS is membership in a local church. It is apparently the case, and understandably so, that local church members who become delegates to wider church bodies are generally less parochial in their outlooks than many of their fellow church members, often on journeys of spiritual development themselves, and that the synods which they attend reinforce a global perspective. The differences should not be so quickly overdrawn. Charles Maxfield cites some research on the local church as follows:[9]

> Did this barrage of resolutions have any impact on the local church? In a survey of persons attending Illinois Conference congregations in 1981, only 7,5% of the people rated "participation in racial justice, civil liberties, etc." as a "very important" work of the church. A similar survey in Indiana-Kentucky Conference in 1989 revealed that 62% of the membership knew little or nothing about the national church. In spite of this ignorance, 45% were pleased with the idea of the national church making pronouncements on social issues, and only 24% opposed.
>
> Whether or not they knew about Synod resolutions, UCC people and congregations did apply the gospel to the world around them. In the 1968 survey, 46% of the respondents participated in community organizations, two-thirds of whom saw this as an expression of their Christian faith. A random survey of UCC church members in 1990 reported that 50% had given an hour or more over the past month to help the poor or sick, 17% had given an hour or more to promote social justice, and 27% had participated in a meeting or march in the past year to promote social change. A survey of UCC churches in 2000 reported that 96% of the congregations responding provided some sort of food assistance to the needy in their community.

SUMMARY

The first fifty years of the United Church of Christ reveal a strong tradition of social and ethical teaching and action in the national setting, and of social service in all settings including local churches. It is an impressive record. Maxfield has aptly summarized this history:

> General Synod has addressed hundreds of social issues, almost always taking a socially liberal position. The UCC has consistently striven to bring its behavior into congruence with what it understood to be the gospel. A few issues became persistent and generated discussion throughout the church. With these persistent issues, the denomination engaged in serious Bible study and theological reflection, and in the cases of Peace and Sexuality produced pioneering theological statements.[10]

NOTES

1. The original report is in Appendix 13 to the Minutes, pages 167-70; the revised Call is Appendix 13A, 171-75.
2. Maxfield has tallied the average from 1973 through 1991 in *A Pilgrim People: A History of the United Church of Christ and its Antecedents* (Cortland, NY: Maxfield Books, 2005), 277. A comprehensive list of actions with abstracts through 1992 is *The Prophetic Vision: Social Policy Statements United Church of Christ General Synods 1957-1992*, published by the Office for Church in Society. Since then a set of abstracts was published after each General Synod, more recently annually by Justice and Witness Ministries: the *2005 Briefing Book*, etc. Indices of General Synod actions have also been published by the office of the Associate General Minister.
3. A Peace Theology Development Team was commissioned and produced a book and study guide, *A Just Peace Church*, Susan Thistlethwaite, ed. (New York: United Church Press, 1986).
4. See FWC president Bob Thompson's article in *United Church News* XXII no. 4 (August/September 2006), A5.
5. Macquarrie, *Principles of Christian Theology*, 2nd ed. (New York: Scribner, 1977).
6. Monika Hellwig, a Roman Catholic theologian, elaborated that point in *Whose Experience Counts in Theological Reflection?* (Milwaukee: Marquette University Press, 1982).
7. See Farrer, *The Glass of Vision*, 2nd ed., (London: Dacre Press, 1956); Hart, *Unfinished Man and the Imagination* (New York: Herder & Herder, 1968).
8. Randi Jones Walker devotes a whole chapter to "The Entertainment of Doubt" in her recent *The Evolution of a UCC Style: Essays in the History, Ecclesiology, and Culture of the United Church of Christ* (Cleveland: United Church Press, 2005).
9. Maxfield, *Op. cit.*, 277-78, with sources documented.
10. *Ibid.*, 289.

THEOLOGICAL WORLDS IN THE UNITED CHURCH OF CHRIST

Collision, Chaos, or Complementarity?

Lee Barrett

The United Church of Christ has been accused of theological vacuity and doctrinal amnesia, often being dismissed as "Christianity light" or the "Untied Church of Christ." Frequently the complaint is that the UCC has substituted the uncritical evocation of religious sentiment or political fervor for rigorous theological reflection. As Roger Shinn has observed, critics have scoffed that theology in the United Church of Christ is little more than "a series of ad hoc opinions usually added on to some practical concern," with "an occasional invocation of biblical and doctrinal proof texts on a basis of convenience."[1] According to some critics, this alleged tendency to use theology to justify positions adopted for ulterior reasons is rooted in the UCC's antiquated habit of regarding the truth of certain religious experiences and socio-political values as being self-evident. According to the UCC's detractors, the naïve "modernist" belief that the meaning of concepts like "love" and "justice" is immediately clear to all right-thinking people dissuades the denomination from engaging in any serious theological conversation that presupposes the contested nature of all religious convictions.

This caricature misdescribes the actual theological situation in the UCC. The problem with the UCC is not a paucity of theology, but is rather an embarrassment of theological riches. A kaleidoscopic superabundance of theology has characterized the UCC from its inception, generated by the irenic experiment of uniting four very different traditions and a multiplicity of "hidden histories." Inspired partly by the Reformed view that God transcends all human efforts to formulate divine truth, the UCC has exhibited a commitment to the revelatory freedom of the Holy Spirit and has resisted

Lee Barrett serves as Professor of Systematic Theology at Lancaster Theological Seminary and is a co-editor of Prism.

the definition and enforcement of doctrine by a coercively authoritative ecclesial magisterium. As a venerable UCC mantra puts it, creeds and confessions function as testimonies, not as tests, of faith to guarantee doctrinal uniformity.

As a wedding of very different ecclesial traditions, the United Church of Christ has always been hospitable to a variety of very divergent theologies. Interestingly, the individual components of this variety do not neatly correlate with the different heritages of the four major predecessor denominations of the UCC, for they were already flourishing in each of the ancestor traditions. In spite of this shared ancestry in each of the predecessor denominations, these trajectories are so different that they may be said to constitute different "theological worlds,"[2] animated by different visceral hopes and fears. Each world revolves around a different assessment of humanity's most fundamental problem, proposes a different form of ultimate satisfaction, and encourages a different type of religious experience. Each one has practiced a different theological method, corresponding to the specific passions that propel it. Each one has construed the essence of Christianity differently, with different understandings of God, Christ, humanity, and salvation. Each one has left an enduring legacy, evolving over time, sometimes waxing and sometimes waning, but showing no signs of disappearing. This essay will attempt to sort out the major differences among these worlds and trace a bit of their histories. The nature of each world is not primarily evident in the type of arguments advanced to defend their respective claims, or even in the doctrinal propositions that typify them. Rather, the essential features of these worlds are most clear in the imagery that informs them, the vocabulary that structures them, and in the rhetorical strategies that advance their purposes. In identifying these worlds, the nature of the assumed audience, the voice of the writer/speaker, and the underlying affective mood are just as important as the explicit theological affirmations. Attending to these features leads to a somewhat different classification system than the older and somewhat misleading categories of "conservative," "liberal," "neo-orthodox," "fundamentalist,' etc., and more easily accounts for the porous nature of the boundaries between them. In order to illumine the distinctive characteristics of these worlds, this essay will examine the work of ecclesial leaders and theologians who have been influential in the public life of the United Church of Christ, often serving on crucial committees, organizing movements, and generating denominationally sponsored writings.

THE WORLD OF ESTRANGEMENT AND RECONCILIATION

One of the most prominent and pervasive theological worlds in the history of the UCC is animated by the dialectic of "estrangement" and "reconciliation," terms which recur with regularity in the works of its proponents. Here the central problem afflicting humanity is alienation and hostility, for individuals have cut themselves off from God, from the cosmos, from the human community, and from themselves.[3] Social groups have fared no better, but have constructed formidable barriers of suspicion and enmity across the globe. Without grace, citizens of this world are lonely, haunted by the suspicion that the universe may be indifferent or unfriendly.[4] The craved resolution is the demolition of all the barriers of fear, guilt, and selfishness that isolate individuals from God and one another so that a cohesive cosmic community, vibrant with mutual affection, trust, and delight, can flourish. Humanity yearns for an ultimately secure and intimate environment in which the polarities of finite/infinite, self/other, and Creator/creation are experienced not as dichotomies but as complementarities. In describing the human problem, the rhetoric of this world is disjunctive, juxtaposing polar opposites in order to set the stage for the resolution of the dialectical tensions. The good news is that God, who alone has the power to heal these divisions, is at work in individual lives, in human history, and even in nature transmuting division into unity-in-difference, a process that will be consummated either in the temporal future or beyond time. All reconciliation at the horizontal level of human society must be rooted in a more fundamental reconciliation at the vertical level with God. Exemplars of this world have gone by many names, none of them adequate, ranging from "neo-orthodox" to "post-liberal." Often it has been associated with the orientation of Karl Barth and Emil Brunner, although its scope is much broader, including many who would otherwise be labeled as evangelicals or neo-liberals. This theological orientation encompasses the Christocentric pietists of the Evangelical Synod, who in some instances were more indebted to Schleiermacher than to Barth, as well as the proponents of the Mercersburg movement, whose theology predated Barth. Many of the architects of the UCC, including most of the authors of the *Statement of Faith* shared this world, guaranteeing that its language would be very prominent in the denominations' founding documents.

Each theological world possesses a different understanding of the authoritative guidelines and norms for Christian life and faith, and a different understanding of how these guidelines and norms function. Given the profound sense of human incapacity, including cognitive incapacity, this world gives priority to Scripture as the basic source of Christian truth. However, the notion that the words of Scripture are directly identifiable with the Word of God, conveying inerrant propositions about all matters of fact is alien to this world. Rather, the revelation of God to Israel and the early church is mediated through human words and therefore through culturally situated language. When Scripture is used worshipfully and illumined by the Holy Spirit, the human words function as the indispensable vehicle of God's Word. As William Bradley, a professor at Hartford Theological Seminary, observed in 1962, this view of Scriptural authority enabled many UCC members to avoid the extremes of liberalism's reduction of the Bible to an expression of human religious experience and fundamentalism's undialectical identification of the text with the Word of God.[5]

This understanding of Scripture as God's Word in, with, and under human words has a long history in the UCC. Many of these themes were implicit in the article on "Faith" in *The Basis of Union* of 1957 with its declaration that we bear witness to "that faith in God which the Scriptures of the Old and New Testaments set forth," and which we are "duty bound to express in the words of our time as God Himself gives us light."[6] Similarly, the "Preamble" to the *Constitution of the United Church of Christ* affirmed that "it [the church] looks to the Word of God in the Scriptures."[7] This theme has resurfaced in the history of the denomination whenever the appreciation of the authority of Scripture has seemed to be waning. The first Craigville Colloquy held in 1984, organized to promote grassroots theological reflection, expressed concern that listening for God's word in Scripture and the Christian heritage was being neglected, reaffirmed the Bible as "the trustworthy rule of faith and practice," and maintained that "Christ speaks to us unfailingly in the prophetic-apostolic testimony."[8] Similarly, in 1993 the founders of Confessing Christ, a movement initiated to foster "joyful and serious theological work" within the UCC, issued a letter reminding the church of its commitment to "listen to God's Word in Holy Scripture."[9]

In this theological world the church's ongoing life of prayer, proclamation, and service provides the indispensable hermeneutic context for the interpretation of Scripture. The high valuation of the historic confessional and liturgical traditions of the church is evident in the foundational documents, including the *The Basis of Union* which lauds the ecumenical creeds and evangelical confessions of the Reformation.[10] In the same way the Preamble to the *Constitution* and Article V uphold the continuing value of the ancient creeds and insights of the reformers.[11] The Mercersburg Society, founded in 1983, as well as the Order of Corpus Christi, founded in 1987, both emphasize the need to embrace the confessional and liturgical traditions of the ecumenical church as they have evolved through the centuries.[12] The first Craigville Colloquy presented the creeds as aids in interpreting Scripture and appealed to the historic consensus of the church on theological basics.[13] In the 1980's the impact in the seminaries of George Lindbeck's *The Nature of Doctrine* and the "linguistic turn" in philosophy and cultural studies revitalized the appeal to doctrinal traditions, on the grounds that all knowledge and religious experience are culturally constructed and therefore dependent on some inherited conceptuality.[14]

In the world of estrangement and reconciliation this emphasis of the Bible and the confessional tradition has functioned to counteract appeals to the independent authority of individual or corporate experience. This world is deeply sensitive to the ease with which the church can uncritically absorb the "common sense" and values of the environing society and fall into cultural captivity. This anxiety was evident in the *Statement of Faith* and other founding documents that intentionally echoed the "no other lord" language of the Barmen Declaration and Dietrich Bonhoeffer. In 1979, the Biblical-Theological-Liturgical Group organized by Frederick Trost issued a brief statement warning of the church's bondage to civil religion, bourgeois culture, managerial techniques, and other ersatz authorities that beguile the church away from Scripture and tradition.[15] Along the same lines, in 1983 thirty-nine UCC faculty persons signed "A **Most** Difficult and Urgent Time," expressing fear that theological reflection in the denomination had degenerated into utilitarianism and ideological posturing and calling for more theological grounding for the policies of the church in the gospel as mediated by the confessional heritage.[16] In 1984 the letter of the Craigville Colloquy also cited the Barmen Declaration in calling for theological reflection that avoids identification with any ideology.[17] Similarly, in 1993 the founding document of Confessing Christ summoned the church back to the theological basics in order to prevent subservience to cultural fads.[18]

In this theological world, the meaning of Scripture is often sought in its narrative structure. Scripture is neither a compendium of doctrinal propositions nor a reservoir of evocative symbols expressing the religious experience of ancient peoples. Rather, the Bible recounts the story of God's deeds from creation to consummation. Although the story may not refer in all instances to empirical events in time and space, the pattern of the narrated activity accurately illlumines the true character of God and invites believers to situate themselves in this cosmic epic. This interpretive orientation was inspired partly by the biblical theology movement of the 1950s, epitomized by G. Ernest Wright's construal of the Bible as the recitation of God's mighty acts, and by Karl Barth's interpretive practice, treating Scripture as the portrayal of the unique identity of Jesus Christ. As Roger Shinn has argued, the prominence of narrative hermeneutics was evident in the very structure of the 1959 *Statement of Faith* that reflected the sequence of the "economic" activities of the persons of the Trinity in creation, redemption, and consummation.[19] Similarly, Elmer Arndt[20] and Allen Miller,[21] two influential theologians at Eden Seminary, observed that the statement testifies to God's deeds and thereby invites our response. The missive from the first Craigville Colloquy also described theology as the recital of God's mighty acts.[22] Gabriel Fackre's many books concerning the Biblical "story" have kept this narrative approach to theology in the limelight, giving this theological orientation a new methodological sophistication through the use of literary critical theory.[23]

This foregrounding of God's mighty acts has been inspired by the conviction that the problem of estrangement is so deep and pervasive that only the agency of God can ultimately remedy it. Eschatological images and the language of "new creation" and "consummation" pervade the discourse of this theological world, for humanity must be reassured that God is powerful enough to remove all the daunting obstacles that block intimacy with God. Accordingly, God is described as the ontologically perfect, superlatively powerful "Wholly Other," qualitatively superior to humanity in being and value, whose desire to have fellowship with humanity is purely gratuitous.[24] God is imaged primarily as a strong parent who welcomes back the prodigal, offering intimacy and protection.[25]

When read in this narrative fashion, the fulcrum of the Biblical story is located in the story of Jesus' life, death, and resurrection. The Bible, including the Old Testament, must be viewed from a Christocentric perspective. In much of the literature of this theological world, Christ has been described as the point of contact between divinity and humanity, and therefore the doctrine of the incarnation has been explicitly foregrounded. For Elmer Arndt, the center of Christianity is God's self-giving love enacted in Jesus, for "he is the bridge which God has thrown over the chasm which separates us from God."[26] Apart from Christ, the "infinite qualitative distinction" between God and humanity would leave humanity feeling lost and alone.

This Christocentric sensibility was powerfully operative in the public language of the new denomination in its formative years, as is evident in the description of Christ as the church's "sole head" in the Preamble to *The Constitution of the United Church of Christ.*[27] The importance of the doctrine of the incarnation (although without the conceptuality of "nature" and "person") is implied in *The Statement of Faith's* affirmation that in Jesus Christ God "has come to us and shared our common lot."[28] Elmer Arndt's small pamphlet on the *Statement of Faith* declared the doctrines of incarnation and reconciliation to be the foundational tenets of the church.[29] Similarly, in 1962 Douglas Horton described Jesus as God's entry into human life in order to disclose God's self and impart a share of the divine life.[30] This Christocentrism has endured in the denomination, becoming explicit whenever the centrality of the person and work of Christ has seemed to have been jeopardized. The letter of the first Craigville Colloquy reminded the church of its Christocentric nature and elaborated the ethical and social consequences of this incarnational orientation.[31] Similarly, the General Synod of 2005 resoundingly reaffirmed the confession that Jesus Christ is sovereign over the church and reaffirmed the cross, crown, and orb as symbols of the denomination.

The Christological focus undergirds the construal of Christ's work as the "reconciliation" necessary both because of the ontological gap separating the Creator and the creature and because of the barrier that sin has erected between humanity and God.[32] The language common in this world suggests that the condition from which we are saved is not so much God's retributive justice as it is self-imposed isolation from God and neighbor, motivated by the simultaneously anxious and prideful desire to secure our own private well-being in a seemingly indifferent universe. The movement of the Christian life is from self-generated estrangement from God to joyous reincorporation into God's family. God's gracious enactment of solidarity and intimacy with humanity was basic for most of the leaders of the founding generation.[33] Accordingly, the theological principles articulated in 1961 for the new UCC curriculum stressed the good news of God's love that heals the breach and restores relationship with God.[34]

In all of this early literature, metaphors of intimacy between God and humanity abounded, suggesting that the reconciling God takes the lonely into fellowship, awakens trust in the anxious, and reassures the discouraged.[35] The Christian life in this world is typically described as an "I –Thou" encounter with God in Christ, a personal relation of such extraordinary value that it confers meaning on all of life.[36] Allen Miller maintained that God does not reveal truths about God's self, but rather manifests God own loving personhood. In this world God is not an object to be known but a mysterious presence to be acknowledged with appreciation, commitment, awe, and wonder. Faith, this profound trust in God's empathy, is certainly not produced by the human spiritual quest for transcendence, but is elicited by God's initiative through the Holy Spirit, from which flow all godly virtues, values, and actions. Out of gratitude, the reconciled individual will embrace a reconciling way of life. Faith is the indispensable root of the joyful obedience whose fruit is the pursuit of shalom.

Given this world's focus on reconciliation, the church is described primarily as a community that celebrates the removal of all barriers between humanity and God.[37] The word "fellowship" recurs regularly to characterize the essence of the church.[38] As Robert Paul observed, "...our ecclesiology must point to the Incarnation of Jesus Christ, or it will compromise its essential testimony . . . it is to point to a **communal expression of what God revealed to us about the divine nature in Jesus Christ.**"[39] Because the message of reconciliation seems counter-intuitive, the church's mission must involve the explicit proclamation of the surprising news of God's love for the alienated world. As a witnessing community, the church's own instantiation of communal care and concern is a witness to God's relatedness to all human beings.[40] This evangelism by means of both word and deed presupposes that the message of reconciliation is both explicitly taught and also caught from those already celebrating it.

Among the heirs of the Mercersburg movement this connection between the doctrine of reconciliation and ecclesiology has been expressed even more strongly and was given institutional form through the founding of the Mercersburg Society in 1983. Proponents of this sacramental and incarnational spirituality have typically stressed the organic union of the church with Jesus, made accessible through the church's central act of worship, the Eucharist, and all Christians' common baptism into Christ's one body.[41] Fragmentation is overcome through incorporation into the body of Christ, the foundation of all reconciliation. The Mercersburg tradition's expansive ecumenical vision is rooted in its core convictions about the reality and power of the incarnation rather than in any Enlightenment-style toleration. The unity of the church is not the product of a shared quest for justice or of a common religious experience, but is grounded in Christ's very real presence in it. In the Mercersburg tradition the language of reunion and home-coming becomes extravagant. The reconciling work of Christ in the church will expand beyond the ecclesial sphere and catalyze the healing of the rifts in society, eventually effecting the renovation of the entire cosmos. The whole world will be infused with the love of God and all enmities, all forms of alienation, will be healed.

THE WORLD OF BENEVOLENCE AND REFORM

The theological world of estrangement/reconciliation was by no means the only powerful theological impetus in the new denomination. In fact, some Congregationalists vociferously denounced "neo-orthodoxy" or "the Barthian viewpoint" as an old-fashioned return to an obsession with sin and a consequent failure to support social progress.[42] An equally powerful and persistent stream in the history of the United Church of Christ perpetuated many of the impulses of the older Social Gospel and "modernist" movements in spite of the blows to human self-confidence dealt by two World Wars and the Great Depression.[43] Sometimes labeled "neo-liberal," its central passions were two-fold: the celebration of God's creative benevolence and the commitment to the moral reformation of the individual and society.[44] Of course, the world of estrangement and reconciliation had also stressed the theme of doing God's will in the world, but it had regarded such endeavors as the fruit of God's restoration of friendship. The inhabitants of this world of "benevolence and reform" did not share the experience of an alienation and incapacity so devastating that only the recreation of the human heart by grace and the promise of a new heaven and a new earth could even begin to heal it. For them, the "Barthians" had underestimated the continuing operation of God's creative power in all the processes of nature and history.[45] The theologians of benevolence and reform saw more continuity and less disjunction between God's creative and redemptive work. They did not express a yearning for a cosmic reconciliation of such magnitude that only God's sovereign agency could secure it, but rather felt relatively at home in this created order. However, the theologians of benevolence and reform were troubled by the realization that individual lives have been stunted by fear, shame, and sloth, and that the social order has been poisoned by systems of injustice and selfishness. By refocusing on God's love and creative energy, wayward humanity could begin to overcome these forms of vice. As Daniel Day Williams remarked, "God has lent us a spark of His creative power, so that within limits we control the conditions of our life."[46] These neo-liberals, like their nineteenth-century forebears, were motivated by a sense of being loved by God to strive to grow spiritually and to rehabilitate human society. For them, Jesus' proclamation of God's love for the individual and the "Kingdom" (or "Reign") of God displaced the doctrine of incarnation as the heart of the Christian gospel. Here the powerful legacy of one strand of nineteenth century German theology, that stretching from Albrecht Ritschl through Adolf von Harnack is evident. In the early twentieth century the influence of Ritschl and various German "mediating" theologies was particularly strong at Union Seminary (New York), Oberlin, and Eden Seminary, with the twin emphases of Christ's love for the individual and the imperative to enact the gospel in the public arena. Through exposure to various adaptations of these theologies, several generations of ministers were immersed in the theme that Christianity is not a doctrine but a life of personal sanctification and social reform. However, unlike the (often erroneous) caricature of the nineteenth-century liberals as naïve enthusiasts for human progress and moral prowess, the "neo-liberals" were sufficiently cognizant of human sin to insist that the ultimate remediation of the human predicament does require a special revelation of God's love and internal empowerment by God's Spirit.

This more positive assessment of life in the world has had inevitable and enduring epistemological consequences. Trusting in God's presence in human cultures, the citizens of the world of benevolence and reform have continued the earlier nineteenth century liberal project of reconceptualizing traditional theological concepts in light of modern knowledge and values. Their intended audience has been educated, socially concerned, and largely prosperous participants in the humane traditions of Western culture. For Yale theologian Robert Calhoun, traditional appeals to revelation can only be accepted if they resonate with reason and experience.[47] Although revelation is essential, truth claims based on external authority must be justified by correlating them with the depth dimensions of human experience and culture.[48] Consequently, it has been imperative for these theologians to develop an analysis of the most general dynamics of human experience in order to distinguish enduring, progressive, and healthy values and convictions from culturally relative, reactionary, and pathological ones. Accordingly, the Bible was construed as an expression of the religious experience of ancient Israel and the early church inspired by God's Spirit.[49]

In this correlation of experience and revelation many neo-liberals have perpetuated Ritschl's and Harnack's distrust of metaphysical claims about the universe, preferring to interpret Christianity in terms of ethical striving. Implicitly, they have followed Kant's appeal to "practical" reason in matters of Christian faith, distinguishing science, which deals with matters of fact, from religion, which deals with matters of value. To this disjunction of theoretic and practical reason, the theologians of benevolence and reform have often added a Schleiermacher-like appeal to a dimension of religious feeling underlying all subjectivity. However, not all "benevolence and reform" theologians have sharply distinguished moral and religious experience from metaphysical speculation. Some, unconvinced by the skepticism concerning metaphysical systems spawned by both analytic philosophy and phenomenology, have embraced sweeping interpretations of the universe borrowed from process and personalist philosophers. In their view, human theoretic reason could indeed support Christian values; in fact, the values of Christianity definitely imply a metaphysics. Within the United Church of Christ Daniel Day Williams appropriated the process thought of Charles Hartshorne and Alfred North Whitehead, while Nels Ferré of Andover-Newton modified the personalist metaphysics of Borden Parker Bowne in order to articulate and ground the faith.[50] Theology is the thematization of Christian experience in the light of the most basic dynamics of the universe, which are freedom, change, relationality, and the drive for more complex forms of satisfaction. The ultimate goal in this theological world is to live this life on earth to the fullest, freely actualizing potentialities in the midst of an interactive ecological community. Life is an adventure of self-fulfillment, in which a harmony should obtain between individual aspirations and the needs of others.[51] The Christian life should exhibit love as mutual concern, mutual delight, and the enjoyment of free, creative action in communion with others. Extending this tradition, UCC process theologians David Stowe and Bruce Epperly have sought to bring the spirit of this movement to a wider audience.[52]

The God-language of the benevolence/reform theologians diverged from that of their estrangement/reconciliation colleagues. Rather than describing God in terms of sovereign, gracious power exercised paradoxically through divine self-giving, this movement understood God as a dynamism immanent in the spiritual maturation of individuals and in the evolutionary processes of history and nature. "Spirit" became the most popular designation for God, with "Source of life" as a close second.[53] When describing the sacred, images of internal energy and teleological propulsion abounded.[54] While some interpersonal vocabulary lingered, particularly the frequent citation of Jesus' use of the intimate term "Abba", this language was employed to combat the conception of God as a coercive feudal monarch ruling the cosmos by external fiat. God is more like a facilitator who acts within all creatures, motivating them, empowering them, empathizing with them, and generating novelty.[55] According to Nels Ferré, God is that which "has so ordered and so controls the world that there is a lure for harmony of being in the self and among selves," and which nurtures "co-operative community within the creative resources for common fulfillment."[56] "Love" has been interpreted as the divine intention to promote the well-being of God's creatures. According to Ferré, "God is continuously working in our behalf... God loves all, is always doing what is best for each and for all."[57] This theological orientation tended to shun numinous adjectives to describe God and saw little tension between God's love and God's justice, which is always remedial and restorative. God is not described as perfect aseity or immutability, but as the universal power of creative mutuality vivifying all things and luring them forward.

In this world Christ as the embodiment of love reveals both the depths of God's benevolence and the glorious possibilities that God intends humanity to actualize.[58] Consequently, the vocabulary used to describe the significance of Christ shifts from ontological language concerning the dramatic bridging of the gap between the finite and the infinite to language suggesting the revelation of perennial aspects of the nature of God and humanity. This revelation is not the mere communication of information, but is an evocative transmission of the "spirit" of Christ. The rhetorical strategies employed by writers in this theological world have attempted to convey a sense of Christ as a living power who reveals the character of God as creative love.[59] Most of these theologians preferred a psychological or agential model of incarnation, locating the presence of God in Jesus' spiritual experience or in Jesus' pattern of action. For theologians like Daniel Day Williams, Jesus' human life was so in tune with God's intentions that it manifests what the love of God looks like. The cross does not so much effect reconciliation as it discloses the empathic depths of God's love, a love that is willing to suffer with and for humanity.[60] Because this Christology did not involve unverifiable claims about the "natures" in Jesus, it could ally itself with the second and third quests for the historically reconstructed Jesus. For many, the interest was not so much in what Jesus taught about specific matters, but rather in the broader values that he inspired, particularly his devotion to the Kingdom. The focus on Christ as the revealer of human possibilities had both an individual and a corporate dimension, enabling these theologians to perpetuate the ethos of the Social Gospel.

In this theological world, sin has been typically defined as the elevation of self-protective and self-aggrandizing proclivities above the imperative to love, a spiritual distortion rooted in a fear-based unwillingness to be open to the full impact of God's love.[61] This self-protective tendency infects both the heart of the individual and the social structures that encourage competition, aggression, and acquisitiveness. The deleterious social environment reinforces the individual's tendency to pursue a life dominated by self-interest, making it fruitless to attempt to sort out the respective culpabilities of the individual and of social groups in the genesis of sin. Although the self-ascription of some responsibility for sin remains, the consequences of sin are felt by the individual not so much as guilt as they are experienced as "emptiness" or "lostness," the failure to find a meaningful direction and center for one's life.[62] In this theological world, the issue of guilt and retributive justice is displaced by the yearning for spiritual health and wholeness.

Consequently, salvation must possess both an individual and a corporate component; it must include both personal regeneration and social reform. The individual must experience the enlivening spirit of Christ, and be filled with an appreciation of the intrinsic value and worth of every individual. This, of course, requires a sense of being valued by God in spite of past lapses, and of being welcomed by God as a contributing agent to God's projects in the world. Salvation has been conceived not so much as a transformation of the individual's relationship with God or objective status, but rather as a subjective transformation in the individual's experience of God and in the individual's system of values. In general, a psychological model of redemption replaced an ontological one. The Christian life that flows from this is not governed by general laws and regulations, but by the spirit of love that must manifests itself in different actions in different specific situations.[63]

Of course, in this world the message of Christianity involves not only the regeneration of the soul but also the reformation of the social world. The introjection of the value system of Jesus into the individual's heart catalyzes a yearning for the actualization of the Kingdom of God. Reformist efforts flow naturally from the love neighbor, for if the neighbor is suffering because of deleterious political and economic structures, the regenerated Christian is obligated to strive to transform them through communal action. The spirit of Jesus is operative in the slow, gradual, and erratic building up of God's Kingdom. Writers in this world have cautioned that this focus on social transformation does not obviate the need for personal transformation, for a prosperous, egalitarian society without regenerated individuals would be nothing more than the triumph of corporate hedonism.

In this theological world the church is understood to be a conduit of

God's revitalizing energy, a fellowship of love, and an agent for change in the contemporary world.[64] God's love for humanity should be incarnated in the corporate experience of the living, historical community of faith. With the spirit of the Kingdom proclaimed by Jesus suffusing congregational life, the church should function as God's task force in the world, characterized by openness to "new ideas" and "progressive values."[65] The church is a kind of revolutionary elite, God's moral and political avant garde. This tradition of activism, shared with other theological worlds, became ingrained in the ethos of the United Church of Christ. In 1959 the UCC Council for Christian Social Action issued "A Call for Christian Action in Society" attacking racism, supporting the United Nations, championing human rights, and demanding the reduction of armaments, all in response to God's activity in history and the love commandment.[66] Continuing this theme, in 1967 the "Statement of Purpose and Mission" by the Committee on Structure identified the church with its mission to "declare that God is at work in the world and to be his servants in the service of men, to meet human need, to undergird institutions of freedom, to preserve human values, and to effect the social change required to secure justice and freedom for all men."[67]

Of course, the social vision of this theological world was by no means monolithic; the understandings of justice and the strategies necessary to implement it diverged and evolved. Back in the 1930s a rift had already developed between those who remained optimistic about the moral reformation of individuals and society, and those who, chastened by war and the Great Depression, were becoming more pessimistic about human nature and its prospects. While admitting that unjust systems make it difficult for individuals to behave virtuously, some theologians like Daniel Day Williams and Douglas Horton continued to advance rather optimistic projects for the Christianization of the church and society. In opposition to this sensibility Reinhold Niebuhr became the public face of the less sanguine camp, objecting that the older "liberal' theology had failed to appreciate the depths of human sinfulness, and had consequently succumbed to an unrealistic utopianism.[68] In a fallen world, politics will always involve the struggle of human groups for power, rendering idealistic projects based on moral suasion ineffective and often dangerous. Although love may be the Christian ideal, more pragmatic calculations of achievable justice should guide Christian decisions about public policy. Although the differences between relative optimists and relative pessimists concerning the assessment of human nature ran deep, both parties shared the conviction that the purpose of Christianity is to cooperate with God's purposes in the world.

THE WORLD OF OPPRESSION AND LIBERATION

Within a decade of the birth of the United Church of Christ, yet another theological world had emerged, equally intent upon the transformation of society. Although it shared the concern for social justice typical of the previous theology, its passions, rhetoric, intended audience, and voice differed markedly. The previous theology had aimed at the spiritual regeneration of individuals in order to mobilize their moral energies for the transformation of society. In so doing, it assumed that its audience enjoyed a position of sufficient social power to have an impact on the dynamics of history. Its literary strategies were designed to foster a sense of altruistic concern in response to the personal experience of God's love. When expositing the story of the Good Samaritan, it identified with the Samaritan, rather than with the victim. The world of benevolence and reform exhibited a middle-class perspective, convinced that the quest for a sense of life's meaning and value is the well-spring of behavior and social change. However, as the 1960s progressed, marginalized groups who had been the objects of altruism demanded to be heard. The civil rights movement itself shifted from the language of "integration" to the language of ethnic pride and identity. The old rhetoric of universal human values and experience was displaced by a new discourse celebrating the irreducible particularities of race, gender, ethnicity, and culture. To these constituencies, solidarity, survival, and empowerment in the face of social victimization were more central than generalized altruism. Their communicative style became more provocative and conflictual as the language of liberation displaced the language of redemption and reconciliation. Attention was directed away from the spiritual transformation of individuals and the amelioration of social ills to the action of God in the struggle for justice. The older implicit concentration on the mobilization of the privileged for benevolent action gave way to attention to the poor as the agents of transformation in history. The demand that the poor should have a voice redirected theological reflection away from issues of growth in benevolence to analyses of the ways that the situation of the poor is structured by baneful historical dynamics and to strategies for the empowerment of human groups. This political emphasis could not be a mere addendum to the theological task, relegated to a subordinate position in social ethics, but demanded the revision of every traditional theological doctrine, from God to eschatology. From this perspective, the perceived theological conservatism of both the Social Gospel and Christian realism with their limited political goals merely reinforced the functioning of the current system. The mood of urgency also spawned a fear that the denomination's concern for ideological pluralism and the desire to be ecumenically sensitive might dampen the zeal for social transformation. The old yearning for ecclesial unity must not be allowed to muffle the cries for justice.

An early intimation of this new theological style was evident in the 1966

"Washington Consultation of Negro Clergymen of the UCC" that met to respond to the black power movement and called for a more forceful voice within the church and society.[69] By 1983 racial and ethnic minorities within the UCC had formed COREM to articulate their perspectives. This concern was emphasized through a variety of public documents and events, including Dean of the School of Divinity of Howard University Lawrence Jones' critique that the UCC *Statement of Faith* was not sufficiently clear about Jesus' identification with the victims of systemic sin.[70] The 1985 manifesto of Christians for Justice Action was saturated with the language of solidarity with the poor.[71] Even more dramatically, in1987 the "Houston Statement on Mission" called the church to join the oppressed in their struggle for liberation.[72] This impetus toward more emancipatory ways of doing theology was both strengthened and rendered more complex by feminist cries for justice in matters of gender. By 1985 Sharon Ringe was drawing attention to the sheer multiplicity of new feminist voices in the UCC, arguing that even feminist theology was no single thing.[73] Native Americans, Asian Americans, Latinos, Latinas, gays, lesbians, and many other cultures and populations added their unique voices to the exhortation to do theology from the concrete situations of oppressed and marginalized people.

These voices within the denomination increasingly influenced the rhetoric of theology in the national setting of the UCC and in the seminaries. In the early 1970s Frederick Herzog and M. Douglas Meeks began exercising and promoting the method of Latin American "liberation theology," calling the church to do theology in solidarity with the poor for the purpose of societal transformation.[74] In 1978 "Toward the Task of Sound Teaching" prepared under the auspices of the Office for Church Life and Leadership declared unequivocally that God sides with the poor and defined the church as a people called to share in God's struggle for justice.[75] The paper exhibited a rather prevalent convergence of the neo-orthodox distrust of culture and liberation theology's suspicion of middle-class piety, a confluence culminating in the demand that the UCC not function as the court chaplain of civil religion. In 1985 the language of Latin American liberation theology informed the UCC's self-identification as a "just peace church" that stood in solidarity with the oppressed.[76]

All the diverse forms of liberation theology embraced an understanding of theological method as critical reflection on praxis. As Roger Shinn and Frederick Herzog insisted, theology must begin with the experience of the poor and clarify this experience of suffering through an analysis of the conditions of oppression.[77] Of course, the situation of oppression and the hope for transformation must be considered in the light of Scripture, and vice versa. In this version of the hermeneutic circle, contemporary political context and text must be read together, with the aim of inspiring and informing transformative action. The dangerous memories encoded in Scripture can unleash a buoyant zeal for participating in God's on-going project to fashion a society of shalom on earth. When the epistemological priority of the oppressed is honored, the Bible can be read in a non-ideological way. Such a perspective protects the reader from the deleterious sexist, racist, and imperialist messages that suffuse the text. For example, Sharon Ringe maintained that authority resides in the textual motifs that encourage resistance to systems of domination, not in those that distort the full humanity of women.[78] Most liberationist thinkers have remained confident that the most foundational themes in the Bible do support the empowerment of the marginalized and not their exclusion.[79]

Although the world of oppression and liberation does correlate text and context, it does not rely upon an analysis of any putatively universal human experience, as did the world of benevolence and reform.[80] For example, the proponents of liberation have not been interested in existentialism's dialectical of angst and authenticity that allegedly informs all human subjectivity, regardless of the particularities of the socio-political situation. These new theological voices rejected such universalizing claims of the bourgeois subject. In their view, the situated nature of all discourse, the positionality of all language, restricts theology to speech from particular contexts. By the 1980s some proponents of this theology had begun to emphasize the theme of the particularity of epistemic contexts so much that they became suspicious of any universalizing theories or programs, even those apparently liberating. Womanists like Valerie Russell, and some feminist theologians objected that the notion of universal female experience is really an attempt to make the experience of white, middle-class women normative.[81] Many newer emancipatory theologians, using the thought of Foucault and post-structuralist theory, have argued that such essentialist reductionism is itself the source of most oppression.[82] Pragmatic local visions of human flourishing, always on behalf of those denied power in particular contexts, should replace the grand world-historical narratives of liberation.

In these various theologies of liberation, God is described in dynamic and agential language, as the generative source of life, battling injustice and all the powers and principalities that block human flourishing. When God is personified, God appears as a sort of senior partner in the co-operative struggle to create a society of love, peace, and justice.[83] God is often described as the creator who does not want to be alone, but freely limits God's power, making room for humanity to share in the sorrows and joys of responsible creativity. At all costs, God must not be construed as a cosmic despot whose tyrannical authority suspiciously resembles that of a human oppressor.

In these theologies attention is directed away from the individual dynamic of sin/sanctification to the more corporate, systemic dimensions of human evil. Sin is embodied in all social structures that turn people into commodities and deny them the opportunity for responsible agency. Pernicious social dynamics like sexism and racism hurt both the oppressor and the oppressed by destroying the possibility of shalom and generating mutual hostility and anxiety. Because such dynamics make it easy for individuals to develop vicious habits and distorted values, the key to the spiritual health of all individuals, relationships, and communities is the transformation of the entire social system.

In this theological world Jesus is usually conceived as the human being who enacted the way of life appropriate to the reign of God. Consequently, the presence of God in Christ should be reconceptualized with agential rather than ontological or psychological categories. God was present in Jesus's praxis in that Jesus performed the liberating acts of God. By so doing Jesus functions as the definitive demonstration of God's solidarity with the poor and the ground of the hope that a just, peaceful society is a genuine possibility. Jesus' willingness to call sinners to participate in God's emancipatory projects reveals God intention to forgive, liberate, and empower all who will respond to God's call for justice, in spite of past complicity in oppression.

Salvation in the world of conflict and liberation is not primarily forgiveness, or the overcoming of a sense of alienation, or growth in holiness, but is rather the transformation of the social world and therefore also the transformation of the network of persons who inhabit it. Forgiveness is God's willingness, reflected in a corresponding human willingness, to allow the past to be truly past so that a new socio-political reality can emerge. Salvation involves hopeful participation in God's work in the world, emboldened by the Holy Spirit, in which a penultimate sense of fulfillment and dignity is found in the struggle itself. The Christian hope is directed toward the fruition of the emancipatory project of God in a society of reciprocity and mutuality, in which all people will enjoy friendship with one another.[84]

This orientation dramatically reconceptualized the understanding of the nature and purpose of the church as an intentional community of transformative praxis.[85] Avoiding any suggestion of corporate Pelagianism, the church is envisioned as a community of resistance and solidarity called forth by God out of nothing. Differing somewhat from the view of the older liberals, the church in this view is not so much God's converted and inspired revolutionary elite as it is the loyal and co-suffering companion of all genuinely emancipatory movements throughout the globe. The church provides material support and spiritual depth, courage, and hope to all who oppose injustice.

THE WORLD OF SIN AND REDEMPTION

A fourth major theological world, often loosely named "evangelical," has been continuously present in the history of the United Church of Christ. This world is animated by the twin dialectics of sin and salvation and of chaos and order. While the boundary between this world of "sin and salvation" and the world of "reconciliation" has often been porous, the citizens of this theological world have typically highlighted the phenomenon of "metanoia," the heart-felt experience of God's forgiving love that transforms the individual's spiritual life. This evangelical impetus had been present in each of the predecessor traditions and was articulated in the early days of the denomination by such UCC leaders as Willis Elliott and Henry Yorden.[86] The voice of this world could be heard in the recurring calls for more attention to piety and evangelism in order to balance and ground the social activism of the 1960s. A similar spirit animated the formation of the UCC Charismatic Fellowship in 1977 that affirmed evangelism in word and deed, the significance of the gifts of the Spirit, and the centrality of an experiential personal relationship with Jesus Christ. In a different guise, this theological sensibility motivated the organization of United Church People for Biblical Witness in 1978 in response to the perceived erosion of Biblical authority.[87] In 1983 the group formulated the Dubuque Declaration and reorganized as the Biblical Witness Fellowship, reconceiving its task as the mobilization of a grass-roots constituency rather than as the lobbying of the denominational leadership.[88]

The proponents of the world of "sin and redemption" have championed a high view of Biblical authority. Like the neo-orthodox party, they remain deeply suspicious of appeals to the authority of experience, fearing that this would engender bondage to the cultures of either the left or the right. Most UCC evangelicals have not equated the sentences of scripture with revelation and have rejected assertions of the faultlessness of the historical recording in Bible. Avoiding the inerrantism of Carl Henry-style fundamentalism, the *Dubuque Declaration* affirms only the infallibility of the Bible as a rule of faith and practice and makes no mention of inerrancy.[89] In spite of being a human book, with human limitations, Scripture is also a divine text.[90] It is culturally conditioned regarding its form, but culturally transcendent regarding its content, being more like a prism of God's truth than like a mirror. The Bible only becomes translucent to revelation when the Holy Spirit works to illumine the reader and the text. Because of the shared Christocentric way of reading Biblical narrative, UCC evangelicals could often find more hermeneutic common ground with Barthians than with scholastic fundamentalists. Some theologians of this world have even expressed fears that fundamentalism has been infected with the spirit of modernity, particularly the habit of treating the Bible as a collection of empirical data from which theological conclusions could be generated through the application of a rigorous inductive method. Nevertheless, the evangelicals differentiate themselves from what they take to be the "neo-orthodox" position that the Bible is a non-propositional human witness to God's saving acts in history, as well as the "post-liberal" view that Scripture functions as a cultural-linguistic framework for interpreting life. Over against these themes, UCC evangelicals, while avoiding merely propositional views of revelation, have usually maintained that Scripture does disclose divine messages that have metaphysical implications. Although revelation is not to be reduced to a set of propositions, revealed theological truths and moral principles can be stated in propositional form, even though these propositions cannot be perfectly organized in a neat deductive system.

For the advocates of this theological world, God's power, sovereignty, and righteousness are emphasized as essential divine attributes.[91] Given the acute sense of the world's fallen nature, the accent must fall on divine power sufficiently potent to rectify the damage. God is the awesome creator and governor of the universe, forging order out of chaos, enacting the divine purposes in nature and history, and commanding human beings to follow God's directives. God's "holiness," the incompatibility between God and all that is unclean or disordered, is often emphasized as a divine attribute that is different from human conceptions of love.[92] The good news for fallen creatures is that God is not only holy and righteous, but also loving and forgiving. Consequently, law and gospel, sin and grace, justification and sanctification become the axes around which this theological world turns.[93]

Sin casts a long shadow over this world; the problem of guilt is one of its most tormenting worries. All individuals and societies are prone to rebel against God's principles and purposes, preferring their own self-will to the glorification of God and the good of the whole. Rather than interpreting sin primarily as a blockage in the relationship with God (although this theme is certainly present), this world more typically emphasizes the culpable violation of God's principles and the incompatibility of God's righteousness and human rebellion. Tragically, this sinfulness infects the deepest recesses of the human heart, distorting all inclinations, and transmitting itself from generation to generation.[94] While individual acts of vice must be evaluated and condemned, the human situation will not improve through the regulation of specific behaviors. The recalcitrance of sin can only be overcome through a transformation of the individual's basic orientation and motivational core.

Given our sinful predicament, the work of Christ must be two-fold. Christ must be the one who secures forgiveness through an atonement that restores the just order of the universe and the one who makes possible moral and spiritual regeneration. In order to accomplish this work, Jesus must possess the power of God that created humanity in the first place and also be the locus in which the restoration of human nature occurs. Because Jesus must be ontologically both divine and human, the incarnation must be highlighted as the necessary condition for the soteriological work of Christ accomplished in the drama of crucifixion and resurrection.

Given the guilt and the debility of sin, our redemption must include both forgiveness (justification) and spiritual/moral healing (sanctification). The *Dubuque Declaration* declares that we are not only saved by Christ's sacrificial atonement, but we are also empowered for justice.[95] Most citizens of the sin/redemption world stress the need for the creation of a new set of passions in the depths of the soul through an experiential union with Christ. Against the perceived liberal reduction of religion to social activism, theologians in this camp often object that the pursuit of justice requires the transformation of the heart, not just new policies and programs that will accomplish nothing without inward spiritual regeneration. Once the union with Christ in faith is operative, the power of Christ's righteousness enables the regenerated individual to grow in sincere enthusiasm for obeying God's precepts. Consequently, Jesus' words and deeds function as an example to be joyfully emulated. The non-ceremonial laws of the Old Testament, the exhortations of the prophets, and the admonishments of Paul also serve as sources of moral principles in the struggle against rebellion and chaos. Accordingly, many inhabitants of this world exhibit an intense concern for specific Biblical regulations, including those pertaining to sexual behavior.

For theologians in the world of sin/redemption, the church's main responsibility is to broadcast the good news of Jesus Christ to the world in order to awaken faith, transform lives, and promote obedience to the principles of righteous living in every sphere of human existence. The church cannot be the church without pursuing the task of evangelism. Many evangelicals have come to fear that the evolution of the UCC has encouraged an idolatry of social-reformist causes, subordinating all aspects of church life to the political dimension. According to the citizens of this theological world, genuine moral passion has degenerated into a self-righteous accommodation to cultural fads and secular ideologies superficially arrayed in religious trappings.

CONCLUSION

No single theological world, no single construal of the essence of Christianity, has ever characterized the United Church of Christ. Several worlds have always thrived, each one with different vocabularies, different moods, different audiences, and different primal hopes and fears. These worlds have sometimes collided, sometimes co-operated, and sometimes formed alliances with one another. The theologians of reconciliation and the champions of benevolence and reform could often agree on the magnitude of God's love revealed in Christ. The theologians of benevolence and reform and the advocates of liberation could often agree that the essential telos of Christianity is the transformation of human society. The theologians of reconciliation and those of salvation have often converged on the centrality of the saving work of Christ. All the worlds could unite in being suspicious of the church's potential captivity to bourgeois culture, although they would disagree about exactly which features of the environing culture should be resisted. All could coalesce around specific programs of social amelioration, although they would harbor different motivations and goals.[96] On the other hand, the advocates for reconciliation and the champions of salvation would often find the liberationists to be too narrowly this-worldly, while the liberationists would condemn the others for being too ethereal and escapist. The theologians of salvation would find the other groups to suffer from an insufficient appreciation of God's holiness and order, while the theologians of benevolence and reform would find many of the others inadequately to value God's love manifested in creation and history.

Some have decried this situation, dismissing it as the theological equivalent of the war of all against all, and have longed for a unity based on a commonality of vision. However, another attitude to this theological pluralism has been present in the United Church of Christ, one that embraces the variety and flux as symptoms of health. According to this view, the oneness of the church need not be constituted by a shared set of homogenous religious passions and aspirations, but by a common commitment to engage in a process of mutual admonishment and affirmation. From this perspective theology is construed as a sweeping conversation among ideologically divergent constituencies. The hope is that a healthy cross-fertilization will occur, in which the partial truths and insights embedded in many different perspectives will complement one another and promote a more multi-dimensional grasp of the gospel. Because such a conversation among multiple perspectives has not yet been fully realized, it would be premature for any theologian in the United Church of Christ to declare a *consensus fideorum,* for no such consensus yet exists. Theology must be tentative, humble, and hospitable, seeking to promote the interaction upon which a future fuller vision of the faith will depend.[97]

In different guises such an interactive, pluralist view has periodically resurfaced during the history of the denomination. During its early days many of the ecumenically-mined proponents of the motto "united and uniting" assumed that a rich theological cross-fertilization of the predecessor confessional traditions would occur, without any of them sacrificing their distinctiveness. The ideal was not the reduction of the particular traditions to an anemic lowest common denominator theology. Douglas Horton lauded the theological latitude of Congregationalism because it permitted a variety of theological perspectives to check and balance one another.[98] For many in the founding generation, the goal was neither homogenization nor a relativism of disparate positions, but an interaction of complementary views, each enriching the other. In a statement to General Synod of 1971 John Esch argued that the denomination should promote a diversity of positions on complex social issues, encouraging individuals to think for themselves in an interactive community.[99] In 1986 Reuben Sheares argued that the UCC was based neither on mere toleration nor on a compromise of two very different traditions, but on a willingness to argue in love.[100] In 1985 the deans of the seven seminaries called for a theological journal, which became *Prism,* not to promote a single viewpoint, but to allow a variety of perspectives to interact with one another. The launching of the seven volume *Living Theological Heritage* in 1989 also drew attention to the sheer variety of theological voices in the UCC.

Ecumenical developments supported this view of theology as a continuing conversation. In the 1970s a new appreciation of the significance of doctrinal differences among denominations became widespread. Consequently, ecumenical initiatives like COCU gravitated away from the goal of organic union to that of covenant communion, in which mutual recognition did not require doctrinal agreement. In 1997 the Formula of Agreement among four Lutheran and Reformed denominations celebrated the positive function of some theological differences, seeing the distinctive emphases of the Reformed and Lutheran groups as reciprocally necessary correctives. The theme of "mutual admonition and affirmation" suggested that the Reformed theme of the sovereignty of God beyond human culture should be held in dialectical tension with the Lutheran emphasis of God's solidarity with humanity in Christ and the sacraments. By themselves, the respective traditions could become distorted, with Lutheran solidarity domesticating the presence of God, and Reformed transcendence dissolving God's presence entirely.

Meanwhile, in the academy, several developments converged to promote the notion of theology as dialogue. In the 1980s the first generation of "post-liberals" concluded that the effort to discover some universal essence of religious experience had failed and argued for the irreducible particularity of religions as language-games that construct different intelligible worlds. The second generation of post-liberals extended this theme of particularity to Christianity itself, doubting the conviction that Christianity has been a monolithic, unified linguistic culture. Kathryn Tanner proposed that cultures have porous boundaries and fluid identities, producing diverging, shifting sub-groups held together by loose networks of family-resemblances rather than by a common essence.[101] Consequently it is not possible to talk about "the" Christian theological system or Christian doctrine as a stable set of linguistic rules. The generation that had not been raised in the pervasive pietist ethos of the early twentieth century, as the founders of the denomination had been, found the notion of a common Christian ethos or hermeneutic to be implausible. In the experience of the children of the 1960s and later, Christian theology had always been an on-going conversation among disparate viewpoints.

Perhaps the plethora of construals of the nature of Christianity is not something to be lamented. Given the magnitude of the God that Christians worship, it makes sense that no specific rendition of the Christian "essence" could claim exclusive validity. Perhaps that is why Scripture contains four different gospels, each with their own emphases and perspectives. The church in its wisdom has usually resisted efforts to reduce the multiplicity of stories to a single narrative. Perhaps the essence of what is Christian can be found only in the fissures, dialectical tensions, and centrifugal forces among the divergent interpretations of the good news.

If this is so, the efforts of any of these theological worlds to invalidate the other options should be resisted, even in the name a collective prophetic voice. As Gabriel Fackre has frequently suggested in lectures, theology should be done with the lead end of the pencil, not the eraser. The vitality of the United Church of Christ may reside in the continuing push and pull among these theological worlds.

NOTES

1. Roger L. Shinn, "Searching for the Centerline," *The Living Theological Heritage of the United Church of Christ*, ed. Frederick Trost and Barbara Brown Zikmund (Cleveland: Pilgrim Press, 2007), vol. 7, 414-415.
2. See W. Paul Jones, *Theological Worlds* (Nashville: Abingdon, 1989).
3. See Elmer Arndt, *The Faith We Proclaim* (Philadelphia: The Christian Education Press, 1960), 8-9; Bela Vassady, *Christ's Church: Evangelical, Catholic, and Reformed* (Grand Rapids: Eerdmans, 1965), 52-125; James Wagner, *Incarnation to Ascension* (Philadelphia: The Christian Education Press,1962); Allen Miller, *Invitation to Theology* (Philadelphia: The Christian Education Press, 1958), 67-132.
4. Nevin Harner, et. al, *Our Christian Beliefs* (Philadelphia: The Christian Education Press, 1954), 18-19.
5. William Bradley, "What Does It Mean To Be a Christian?" *The Living Theological Heritage*, vol. 7, 297.
6. "The Basis of Union," *The Living Theological Heritage*, vol. 7,10.
7. "Preamble," *The Living Theological Heritage*, vol. 7, 42.

8. "The Craigville Colloquy Letter," *The Living Theological Heritage,* vol. 7, 334.
9. "Letter from Organizing Committee of Confessing Christ,' *The Living Theological Heritage,* vol. 7, 389-390.
10. "The Basis of Union: Article II: Faith," *The Living Theological Heritage,* vol. 7, 10.
11. "Constitution of the United Church of Christ: Preamble," *The Living Theological Heritage,* vol. 7, 42.
12. John Shetler, "What Does Mercersburg Have to Offer?" and "The Order of Corpus Christ," *The Living Theological Heritage,* vol. 7, 368-372.
13. "Confessing Christ," *Living Theological Heritage,* vol. 7, 390-391.
14. George Lindbeck, *The Nature of Doctrine* (Philadelphia: Westminster Press, 1984).
15. "A Declaration," *The Living Theological Heritage,* vol. 7, 333.
16. "A Letter from Thirty-nine...," The Living Theological Heritage, vol. 7, 325-328.
17. "The Craigville Colloquy Letter," *The Living Theological Heritage,* vol. 7, 334-339.
18. "Confessing Christ," *The Living Theological Heritage,* vol. 7, 390-391.
19. Roger Shinn, *Confessing Our Faith* (Cleveland: Confessing Our Faith, 1990), 35-43.
20. Elmer Arndt, "A Brief Introduction to the Statement of Faith," *The Living Theological Heritage,* vol. 7, 22-26.
21. Allen O. Miller, *The United Church of Christ Statement of Faith: A Historical, Biblical, and Theological Perspective* (New York: United Church of Christ Press, 1990).
22. "The Craigville Colloquy Letter," *The Living Theological Heritage.* vol. 7, 334-339.
23. Gabriel Fackre, *The Christian Story* (Grand Rapids: Eerdmans, 1978).
24. Elmer Arndt, *The Faith We Proclaim,* 74-75.
25. Nevin Harner, et. al., *Our Christian Beliefs,* 22.
26. Elmer Arndt, *Op.* cit., 50.
27. "Constitution of the United Church of Christ," *The Living Theological Heritage,* vol. 7, 42.
28. "United Church of Christ Statement of Faith," *The Living Theological Heritage,* vol. 7, 18.
29. Elmer Arndt, "A Brief Introduction to the Statement of Faith," *The Living Theological Heritage,* vol. 7, 22-26.
30. Douglas Horton, *The United Church of Christ: Its Origins, Organization, and Role in the World Today* (New York: T. Nelson, 1962).
31. "The Craigville Colloquy Letter," *The Living Theological Heritage,* vol. 7, 334-339.

32. Elmer Arndt, *Op. cit.*, 51.
33. *Ibid.*, 8-13.
34. "Educational Principles," *The Living Theological Heritage*, vol. 7, 260-268.
35. Elmer Arndt, *Op. cit.*, 8-13.
36. Allen O. Miller, *The United Church of Christ Statement of Faith: A Historical, Biblical and Theological Perspective* (New York: United Church Press, 1990), 35-39; Elmer Arndt, *Op. cit.*, 66-68.
37. Ruben Huenemann, "Need for Dialogue," *Reform and Renewal* (Philadelphia: United Church Press, 1966), 48-57.
38. Elmer Arndt, *Op. cit.*, 128-129.
39. Robert Paul, *Freedom with Order* (New York: United Church Press, 1987), 7.
40. Allen Miller, *Op. cit.*, 35-39.
41. John Shetler, "What Does Mercersburg Have to Offer?" *The Living Theological Heritage*. vol. 7, 370-372.
42. See Theodore Trost, *Douglas Horton and the Ecumenical Impulse in American Religion* (Cambridge: Harvard University Press, 2002), 79-80.
43. See Gary Dorrien, *The Making of American Liberal Theology: Idealism, Realism, & Modernity* (Louisville: Westminster John Knox Press, 2003).
44. David Stowe, "A Fellowship of Christians in the World," *The Church in the World* (Philadelphia: United Church Board for Homeland Ministries, 1965), 186-189.
45. Nels Ferré, *Searchlights on Contemporary Theology* (New York: Harper & Brothers, 1961), 105.
46. Daniel Day Williams, *Christian Teaching and Christian Beliefs* (Philadelphia: United Church Board for Homeland Ministries, 1966), 15.
47. Robert Calhoun, "A Liberal Bandaged but Unbowed," *Christian Century* (May 31,1939), 701-704.
48. Daniel Day Williams, *Christian Teaching and Christian Beliefs*,11-13; Paul Hammer, "A Deepening of Biblical and Theological Uderstanding," *The Church in our World* (Philadelphia: United Church Board for Homeland Ministries, 1965), 17-23.
49. Paul Hammer, *Op. cit.*,11-14.
50. See Daniel Day Williams, *Christian Teaching and Christian Beliefs* (Philadelphia: United Church Board for Homeland Ministries, 1966); Nels Ferré, *Christ and the Christian* (New York: Harper & Brothers, 1958).
51. See Daniel Day Williams, "The Declarations of the Deeds of God," in Daniel Day Williams and Roger Shinn eds., *We Believe* (Philadelphia: United Church Press, 1966), 48-49.
52. See Bruce Epperly, *The Power of Affirmative Faith* (St. Louis: Chalice Press, 2001).
53. Paul Hammer, *Op. cit.*, 12-14; Daniel Day Williams, "The Declaration of the Deeds of God," in *We Believe*, 38-39.

54. Douglas Horton, "Truth in Tension," *Reform and Renewal* (Philadelphia: United Church Press, 1966), 9-23.
55. Daniel Day Williams, *Christian Teaching and Christian Beliefs*, 5-7.
56. Nels Ferré, *Searchlights on Contemporary Theology* (New York: Harper & Brothers, 1961), 49, 51.
57. Nels Ferré, *Know Your Faith* (New York: Harper & Brothers, 1959), 38.
58. Daniel Day Williams, *Christian Teaching and Christian Beliefs*, 8-10.
59. Douglas Horton, *The United Church of Christ* (Glen Rock, N. J.: Paulist Press, 1966), 10-12.
60. Nels Ferré, *Christ and the Christian* (New York: Harper & Brothers, 1958), 141-187.
61. Daniel Day Williams, *Christian Teaching and Christian Beliefs*, 14-16; Nels Ferré, *Know Your Faith*, 48-49.
62. Daniel Day Williams, "The Declarations of the Deeds of God," *We Believe*, 54-55.
63. Nels Ferré, *Christ and the Christian*, 50-72.
64. Douglas Horton, "Truth in Tension," *Reform and Renewal*, 9-23.
65. Gerald Jud, "Identity and Promise," *Reform and Renewal*, 106-119.
66. "Call to Christian Action in Society," *The Living Theological Heritage*, vol. 7, 80-85.
67. "Statement of Purpose and Mission," *The Living Theological Heritage*, vol. 7, 53.
68. See Reinhold Neibuhr, *The Nature and Destiny of Man*, vol. 1 (New York: Charles Scribners, 1941).
69. "Washington Consultation Statement," *Living Theological Heritage*, vol. 7, 110-114.
70. Howard Jones, "Reflections on the Statement of Faith," *The Living Theological Heritage*, vol. 7, 29-32.
71. Christians for Justice Action, "The Prophet Speaks to Our Times," *New Conversations*, (Spring, 1985), 24-25.
72. "Houston Statement on Mission," *The Living Theological Heritage*, vol. 7, 419.
73. Sharon Ringe, "Feminist Theology and the United Church of Christ," *The Living Theological Heritage*, vol. 7, 356-362.
74. Frederick Herzog, *Liberation Theology: Liberation in the Light of the Fourth Gospel* (New York: The Seabury Pres, 1972); Frederick Herzog, *Justice Church* (Maryknoll, New York: Orbis Books, 1980); Frederick Herzog, *God-Walk: Liberation Shaping Dogmatics* (Maryknoll, New York: Orbis Books, 1988); M. Douglas Meeks, "How To Speak to God in an Affluent Society," in *Is Liberation Theology for North America?* (New York: Theologies in the Americas, 1979).
75. "Toward the Task of Sound Teaching," *The Living Theological Heritage*, vol. 7, 318-321.

76. Susan Thistlethwaite, ed., *A Just Peace Church: The Peace Theology Development Team* (New York: United Church Press, 1986).
77. Roger Shinn, "Searching for the Centerline," *The Living Theological Heritage,* vol. 7, 414-416.
78. Sharon Ringe, "Feminist Theology and the United Church of Christ," *The Living Theological Heritage,* vol. 7.
79. Walter Brueggemann, *Living Toward a Vision* (Philadelphia: United Church Press, 1976).
80. Susan Thistlethwaite, *Sex, Race, and God: Christian Feminism in Black and White* (New York: Crossroad, 1989).
81. Valerie Russell, "A Minority Woman's Point of View, *The Living Theological Heritage,* vol. 7, 478-480.
82. See Eleazar Fernandez, *Reimagining the Human* (St. Louis: Chalice Press, 2004), 11-30.
83. Susan Thistlethwaite, "Theological Foundations of the Just Peace Church," in *A Just Peace Church.*
84. Susan Thistlethwaite, *A Just Peace Church,* 51-60.
85. Frederick Herzog, *God-Walk: Liberation Shaping Dogmatics.*
86. Willis Elliott, "What Is the Scribal Mentality?" *The Living Theological Heritage,* vol. 7, 126-130.
87. See Martin Duffy, ed., *Issues in Sexual Ethics* (Souderton, Pa: United Church People for Biblical Witness, 1979).
88. "The Dubuque Declaration," *The Living Theological Heritage,* vol. 7, 346.
89. *Ibid.*
90. Donald Bloesch, *The Essentials of Evangelical Theology* (New York: Harper & Row, 1978), vol. I, 51-78.
91. *Ibid.,* 24-50.
92. *Ibid.,* 32-34.
93. "The Dubuque Declaration," *The Living Theological Heritage,* vol. 7, 346.
94. Donald Bloesch, *Op. cit.,* 88-117.
95. "The Dubuque Declaration," *The Living Theological Heritage,* vol. 7, 346.
96. "A Statement of Commitment," *The Living Theological Heritage,* vol. 7, 136-138.
97. For a parallel conclusion, see Peter Schmiechen, *Christ the Reconciler* (Grand Rapids: Eerdmans, 1996).
98. Theodore Trost, *Douglas Horton,* 60
99. John Esch, "Statement to General Synod," *The LivingTheological Heritage,* vol. 7, 119-121.
100. Reuben Sheares, "The U.C.C.: A Merger of Two Kinds of Churches," *The Living Theological Heritage,* vol. 7, 58-63.
101. Kathryn Tanner, *Theories of Culture* (Minneapolis: Fortress, 1997).

IDENTITY AND IDENTIFICATION:

The United Church of Christ's "God is Still Speaking," Television Ad Campaign

Theodore Louis Trost

Unveiled at the General Synod in Minneapolis in 2003, the "God is Still Speaking," campaign came to widespread public attention during the Advent season of 2004 in the aftermath of a controversy surrounding the airing of the United Church of Christ's first-ever television commercial. This essay traces the development of the ad campaign from its origins in a dream in California through the airing of the second television commercial, mainly on cable television, during the Lenten season of 2006. I offer at the outset an implicit distinction between identity and identification. "Identity," the realm of historians and psychologists, has to do significantly with the past. It is for this reason that Israel of old is constantly called upon to remember, for example, that the people were once enslaved in the land of Israel. This memory when held dearly should lead to acts of justice and kindness in the present and a way of behaving, a way of building community, into the future. "Identification," on the other hand, is directed in particular to those outside of a given community. It has to do with "branding," that is to say, with name recognition. A passport, for example, is a form of identification. It provides inquirers (customs agents; Homeland Security) with the information they need to make certain judgments about the bearer; it provides the bearer herself with almost no useful information about her "true identity." The television ads that are the primary focus of this investigation are means of identification. Whether or not they, like some passports, offer a "likeness" to the church they purport to identify, is one of the many issues the "God is Still Speaking," campaign continues to raise for people inside and outside of the denomination.

Theodore Trost is Associate Professor in Religious Studies at New College and the University of Alabama, Tuscaloosa.

THE ORIGIN OF THE CAMPAIGN

Ron Buford's Dream

In an article in the denomination's *New Conversations* series (subsequently discontinued), Ron Buford and Randy Varcho tell the story of how the "God is Still Speaking," campaign (or The Still Speaking Initiative [TSI]) came into being.[1] They begin with an account of a new age-style dream workshop conducted by the Rev. Wilbur Green at the Plymouth United Church of Christ in Shaker Heights, Ohio. Presumably (though the article does not make this explicit), Buford and perhaps also Varcho attended the sessions. As workshop participants gathered in a circle, a smooth stone would pass from person to person. Each participant would hold this "dream stone" for a while and, before passing the stone on to a neighbor, would "listen" to the stone "with some long dormant and all-but forgotten sense, listening for [one's] own lost and abandoned soul or the lost and abandoned soul of another." Eventually each participant would be called upon to share a dream and, by so doing, "the soul of the original dream was liberated from the stone."[2]

Liberating the dream from the stone becomes a kind of spiritual labor that Buford and Varcho (referring to themselves in the third person) proceed to undertake as they subsequently speak the "God Is Still Speaking" campaign into existence. This story of origins begins by noting in passing an "absentminded" purchase made by Buford (then UCC public relations and marketing manager) in a Los Angeles post card shop while on vacation in mid-2001. Buford admits that he did not actually like the postcard, noting "it was crudely designed and the colors were wrong"; but he purchased it nevertheless because he was drawn to the words on the front: "Never place a period where God has placed a comma." These words, they report, were discovered by actor George Burns among the papers of his wife, Gracie Allen, after her death.[3] Seemingly haunted by Gracie Allen's remark, Buford subsequently awoke at 3 AM "in the quiet of his California bed," and then "suddenly, on the graces of some dormant and all-but-forgotten sense of dream telling, he began to speak."[4]

The elements that converge by coincidence to frame this decisive moment in the history of the United Church of Christ are worth subjecting to an admittedly extravagant reading (in accordance with the theme of "extravagant welcome" that the ensuing campaign will recommend).[5] To begin, there's the reference to the number three which, in the Christian tradition, might suggest the Trinity and more specifically the third person of the Trinity. The Holy Spirit speaks through human beings as witness to the living God, Biblically speaking. This Spirit is also "still speaking" and remarkably so among contemporary Pentecostals, for example—the fastest growing group of Christians in the world today. Sometimes this speaking manifests itself as articulate speech in a manner after the disciples as recorded in the second chapter of Acts; and sometimes "the tongues. . . of angels" speak (as the apostle Paul remarked with reference to the church at Corinth) and a prophet is required to interpret what the Spirit, through the phenomenon of glossolalia, is saying. In any case, Buford and Varcho's account contains this fortuitous conjuration of the Trinity and the movement into speech characteristic of Pentecostalism.[6] The reference to dream-telling, meanwhile, signals a kind of new age spirituality mentioned at the very beginning of the article as having been nurtured under the guidance of an ordained UCC pastor in the context of the Christian community at Shaker Heights. The act of dreaming is also significant and provides a little balance to the extra-traditional resources in play thus far. For Buford's dream bears the weight of the Biblical theme of dreams—the specialty of prophets, notably Joseph and Daniel. Literarily, then (and existentially), the signs are in place for a momentous word to come to and through Mr. Buford.

The words that came to him at that mystical moment were from an old Congregational hymn, slightly altered for inclusion in *The New Century Hymnal:* "O God, grant yet more light and truth to break forth from your word."[7] Buford's first reaction to these words was that they would never fit on a bumper sticker. But then, according to the account, "the dream itself . . . told a bit more: 'God is still speaking,'." [sic: punctuation in the original]. To keep this "anchor of his unfolding dream" in mind, Buford dashed off an e-mail to Randy Varcho, a trusted colleague and a "design genius."[8] As collaborators in a "living dream workshop," Buford and Varcho quickly pieced together the elements of a new identity campaign for the United Church of Christ. These included:

1. The Gracie Allen quote "Never place a period where God has placed a comma"
2. A "huge black comma" on a red background
3. The slogan "God is Still Speaking," (note the comma as a sign of grammatical and social "openness"; the congregations in the UCC that make a specific appeal to and affirmation of lesbian, gay, bisexual and transgendered persons are called "Open and Affirming" congregations)
4. A "gently revised UCC 'brand' that emphasizes 'United Church' and 'of Christ' as distinct phrases"

The "God is Still Speaking," campaign, according to Buford and Varcho, was "conceived as though in a moment of rare and passionate ecstasy."[9] The excitement with which "ever-growing numbers" of people subsequently embraced the message appears to suggest to the campaign's originators that "we have caught creativity from the Divine One, as though it has jumped from our arms, taken form that lives among us for a while."[10] Part of the perceived brilliance of the "God is Still Speaking," campaign, then, is attributable to its congruity with Pastor Robinson's message that more light and truth will break forth from God's word.[11] The authors apparently understand Gracie Allen's words to be in continuity with God's word; moreover, their own inspiration for the campaign is indisputably God-given. But they also think there are practical reasons for the message's success: its open-endedness and "the fact that the genius of the piece lies in its engagingly simple mutability."[12]

This malleable quality of the campaign means that the signifier, the "huge black comma," can be filled with a variety of contents. In the context of the troubled financial state of the United Church of Christ and the need for the "God is Still Speaking," campaign to inspire significant contributions to the church, Buford suggests "an entirely new and helpful meaning" for the Gracie Allen quote. Indeed, he expresses surprise at not catching the "obvious connection" from the start. By this reading, "Never place a period where God has placed a comma" becomes an appeal for extravagant financial underwriting. As Buford and Varcho remark: "With God, every $100 becomes $100,000 . . . and on and on."[13] According to the Buford and Varcho account, then, the "God is Still Speaking," campaign originated in a prophetic dream and the seemingly Spirit-filled experience of Buford himself. It is this experience that convinces Buford that Gracie Allen's comment comes from God and is meant to be significant for the one million plus people who constitute his denomination. Moreover, the success of the vision is guaranteed as the left-leaning commas lean further to the left and hundreds become thousands and ten thousands of dollars.

One critic has likened the language of the campaign itself to Henry T. Blackaby's best selling book *Experiencing God: How to Love the Full Adventure of Knowing and Doing the Will of God*. For example, Blackaby asks: "Does God really speak to His people in our day? Yes! God has not changed. He still speaks to His people."[14] This rhetorical link to evangelical, "gospel of success" Protestantism is ironic and intriguing. Both Blackaby and TSI participate in a kind of optimism that one would welcome. Both boldly advance a language of faith. But it is worth noting in passing that rhetoric like this is also a product of the times. And 21st century Americans have been made particularly sensitive to language that, in another context, speaks over-optimistically about being "welcomed as liberators"; that characterizes a preliminary operation as a "mission accomplished"; that dismisses missteps and cruelties as the actions of "a few bad apples," etc. The proof of the pudding—to resort to another slogan (or cliché)—is in the tasting. By what measure might the "God is Still Speaking," campaign be deemed successful? This is the question, ultimately, that hovers over the entire enterprise.

The Campaign's Debut

The "God is Still Speaking," identity campaign made its official debut at the United Church of Christ's General Synod XXIV, held at Minneapolis in July 2003. At the time the campaign had a number of slogans, graphic art ideas, and a plan that would allow churches to "opt-in" to the ongoing campaign. Congregations that did "opt-in" would be given, among other things, assistance in setting up web pages that would link directly to the national "God is Still Speaking," campaign web site. At the same General Synod meeting, John Thomas, the UCC's General Minister and President, called for UCC members "to increase overall giving to local churches to $1 billion annually by 2007." This call for increased giving was made at a time when, according to projections based on existing trends, "cumulative deficits would mount to an estimated $33 million by 2007."[15] And so, "The Stillspeaking Initiative" arose at a time of financial peril in the UCC. Nevertheless, the denomination's leaders determined that it was worthwhile to undertake the first television ad campaign, and the most expensive identity campaign in the denomination's history, based on a "Field of Dreams" kind of faith: if you build it, they will come. This optimism (or faith) is expressed repeatedly on the denomination's web site and in the "God is Still Speaking," campaign literature. According to Ron Buford, in his role as the denomination's public relations and marketing manager when TSI began: "People are leaving our churches on Sunday morning with pockets full of money giving it to everyone else, because we're not asking for it." All the denomination had to do, Buford seemed to be saying, was ask and the projected deficits would disappear. After all, Buford affirmed, "money really is the language of love."[16]

At the same time TSI was developing, the denomination also inaugurated "The Catalyst Project"—an effort to stimulate church giving, or stewardship, by educating the congregations about the important ministries undertaken by the Board of World Missions. The "Catalyst Campaign" managers convened a meeting of about 80 local church pastors that took place in Cleveland in January 2004. The purpose of this meeting was to increase local giving by at least $140 million by 2007—the denomination's 50th anniversary. According to the campaign's then-interim director, Ron Buford, the denomination needed "to provide greater help to our local churches, who are strapped financially, and the only way forward is to state our case.

We should stop the blame game—'Who's [sic] fault is it that we don't have enough money?'—and start trusting that God is doing a new thing."[17] This faith or optimism expressed in Buford's quote was also central to the "God is Still Speaking Campaign," with Buford as its director. At the time of the meeting in Cleveland plans were already underway to launch the UCC's first-ever major national marketing campaign with runs of a UCC ad in seven local markets to appear throughout the Lenten season (March 1-April 11, 2004). The relationship between the national ad and the Catalyst Campaign, then, was to generate an interest in the national church, to suggest that it was doing good things, and to fortify relations among the various "settings" of ministry throughout the denomination.

PART TWO: THE FIRST SERIES OF CONTROVERSIAL TV COMMERCIALS

The "Bouncer Ad"

On December 1, 2004, the United Church of Christ launched its first-ever, nationwide television advertising campaign. The inaugural 30-second spot, initially called "Night Club" but later dubbed the "Bouncer Ad," features two muscle-bound security guards stationed at the entryway to a tall steeple church. As church bells toll in the background and with ominous synthesized bass notes providing an undertone of foreboding, the bouncers decide whom to admit into the church and whom to exclude from admission. Allowed in are two care-free and smiling teenage girls and their attractive, well-dressed parents: a portrait of the American family (perhaps even suggestive of America's "first family" at the time). Among those kept out are two lean, clean-shaven men holding hands; a Hispanic teenager; an African American girl; and a white man in a wheelchair. The cold gazes of the bouncers collide with looks of disappointment on the faces of those denied entry with words like "not you"; "no"; "no way." A sharp clang like the sound of a slammed iron gate echoes as the picture fades to black.

Next, the music ascends to the treble clef and two sentences appear in multi-colored lettering on the screen: "Jesus didn't turn people away. Neither do we." Congas kick up a kind of world beat; a single voice in an unrecognizable tongue starts singing; soon a whole choir joins in, in sympathetic and celebratory tones. An ecumenical gathering of humanity appears on the screen: old people; young people; red, yellow, black, brown and white people. The camera zooms in on various faces in the crowd: an Asian girl with a white girl; a Hispanic boy; an African American man and woman; an elderly white couple (the woman placing her hand on the man's shoulder with seeming affection); and two white women (one placing her hand on the other's shoulder with seeming affection). While these portraits flash briefly upon the screen, the announcer's voice-over declares: "The United Church [*pause*] of Christ: no matter who you are or where you are on life's journey, you're welcome here." The advertisement ends with a still shot of the UCC's logo in black against a band of red. Above the church's name appears the slogan for this identity campaign, "God it still speaking," and below it in bold letters is the denomination's web site address.[18]

Media Response to the Ad and the Response to the Media Response

The "Bouncer Ad" and another ad called "All of the People" were produced by Gotham Advertising of New York in early 2004 to be aired during the season of Lent (the pre-Easter season of February and March) in select test markets across the United States. This was done in anticipation of a big nationwide advertising campaign during the Christmas season later that same (calendar) year. In advance of the test marketing, the UCC submitted the two ads for approval to the major networks. ABC refused outright to air the ads, claiming that the network had a policy against all religious advertising. The CBS television network sent a fax from Robert L. Lowary on Feb 19, 2004, to Ms. Jena Stadtlander, the person managing the advertising account for the UCC. The message in full reads:

> Approval Withheld
>
> CBS/UPN Network policy precludes accepting advertising that touches on and/or takes a position on one side of a current controversial issue of public importance. Because this commercial touches on the exclusion of gay couples and other minority groups by other individuals and organizations, and the fact that the Executive Branch has recently proposed a Constitutional Amendment to define marriage as a union between a man and a woman, this spot is unacceptable for broadcast on the networks.
>
> While moot, we must advise that CBS/UPN does accept advertising from churches and religious organizations which deliver secular messages that are beneficial to society in general. Nevertheless, advertising that proselytizes on behalf of any single religion is not acceptable. In our view, this commercial does proselytize.[19]

NBC's message was briefer. In her February 19th memo, Theda Browdy circled "clearance must wait" and wrote "too controversial" across the form.

Network approval was not necessary for the Lenten ad campaign since advertising buys were made at local stations in six select markets to begin March 1 and continue through Easter Sunday, April 11. The ads were scheduled to air on network-affiliated, as well as cable, stations in the test markets of: Harrisburg/Lancaster/Lebanon/York, Pennsylvania; Raleigh-Durham/Fayetteville, North Carolina; Oklahoma City, Oklahoma; Springfield/Holyoke, Massachusetts; Tampa/St. Petersburg/Sarasota, Florida; and Cleveland/Akron/Canton, Ohio. The two ads were each designed to take into account the feedback from "almost 200 participants" in nine focus groups held in January. According to J. Bennett Guess, writing in the March 2004 edition of the *United Church News*, the themes of "extravagant welcome and inclusion" were emphasized in both ads because the people in the focus groups "above all. . . wanted a church that welcomed everybody."[20] Guess goes on to say that only the "Bouncer Ad" would air during the Lenten season; both ads would be released for the national audience in the winter.

If, as Bennett Guess seems to suggest, only the "Bouncer Ad" was aired during the test marketing campaign, this means that the "God is Still Speaking," campaign managers, or the UCC's Office of Communications, or both, knew they were choosing to promote the "edgier" of the ads—since the "Bouncer Ad" had already been rejected by the national networks. Presumably, the subsequent marketing research gathered from the Lenten campaign showed that the "Bouncer Ad" did reach the UCC's intended audience. Guess describes this audience as "young adults, especially women, ages 25 to 50 and those with young children." A generous reading of the "Bouncer Ad" could conclude that this audience is also targeted in the ad, but this audience was not interpreted to be its main intended audience by the professional ad reviewers at NBC and CBS.

In any case, the "Bouncer Ad" continued to appear on the "God is Still Speaking," website and extensive promotion for the December roll-out of the national ad campaign was maintained in the denomination's national newspaper and on-line. Apparently, no mention was made anywhere of the networks' rejection of the ad.[21] To the contrary, the denomination's publications led members to believe that "the initial advertising spot" would soon be appearing nationwide.[22] Indeed, in a news release dated November 29, 2004, the denomination focused mainly on the "Bouncer Ad" and announced that the nationwide campaign "expected to reach 60 percent of the U.S. population with edgy crossover ads."[23] On the next day, however, a news release from the "Still Speaking" website announced: "CBS, NBC refuse to air television advertisement: United Church of Christ ad highlighting Jesus' extravagant welcome called 'too controversial.'" While quoting from the memos that had been in the denomination's possession since February, the press release noted that "negotiations between network officials and the church's representatives broke down today (Nov. 30) on the day before the ad campaign was set to begin airing nationwide on a combination of broadcast and cable networks." The release proceeds as if the denomination were taken by surprise by the network's refusal and offers a quote from the Rev. Robert Chase, director of the UCC's communication ministry: "We find it disturbing that the networks in question seem to have no problem exploiting gay persons through mindless comedies or titillating dramas, but when it comes to a church's loving welcome of committed gay couples, that's where they draw the line."[24] In an article written the day after the ad did not appear, the *United Church News* emphasized that "Only recently did UCC learn of networks' ultimate refusal of church ads." But the article does not clarify the nature of the on-going negotiations with the networks in the effort to have the ads aired; indeed, if documents pertaining to these negotiations exist, they have not been made public.[25]

The campaign that followed in response to the "censorship" was directed by Robert Chase from the Office of Communications in Cleveland. The ad was suddenly appearing everywhere, especially at the denominations web site, but also as a news item on many local stations and as a commercial on a variety of cable networks, including CNN. The UCC cried censorship. Meanwhile, the Office of Communication's talking points were reproduced in dozens of newspaper articles and editorials across the country.

Importantly, the UCC ad appeared at a time when other U.S. denominations were experiencing tensions over sexual politics: the expulsion of a lesbian minister from the United Methodist Church; the elevation of a gay Episcopal bishop in New Hampshire; the ordination of "renegade Catholic" women priests on a boat in the Saint Lawrence Seaway; and a program promulgated by the new pope to get homosexuals out of Catholic seminaries. In their memo rejecting the "Bouncer Ad," CBS referred to efforts on the part of the Bush White House to advance a constitutional amendment to define marriage as a union between a man and a woman. The "Bouncer Ad" is one of the UCC's contributions to the larger cultural debate.

Consequences After the First Ad

All of this publicity has not been without reward—or at least consequence. For example, on October 30, 2005, the 4,300 member Cathedral of Hope in Dallas, Texas, voted to affiliate with the United Church of Christ. In an article in the *United Church News*, this congregation was identified as "the world's largest liberal Christian church with a primary outreach to lesbian, gay, bisexual, and transgendered people."[26] If it were to join the UCC (which it subsequently did do), the article asserted, the Cathedral of Hope would become the denomination's third largest church. Meanwhile, the article remarks that news of the Cathedral of Hope's interest in the UCC comes at the same time that "UCC leaders are conceding that an estimated 20 congregations are likely to leave the denomination," presumably in response to the denomination's advocacy of same-gender marriage equality. This news is called "ironic" because at the same time that big new churches such as the Cathedral of Hope are taking an interest in the denomination, other churches that had been linked to the denomination for decades and even centuries are withdrawing. Whether this is "ironic," or "unanticipated," or "strategic" is a matter of more than mere semantics. Clearly, the UCC is attracting some wealthy congregations to the fold. It is worth noting here that the entire "God is Still Speaking," campaign was inaugurated in an effort to bring more financial resources to the denomination. From one point of view, to lose old churches that do not contribute to national initiatives while attracting wealthy new ones that do is a major success.

A second consequence of the "God is Still Speaking," campaign was the announcement that the "Bouncer Ad" received the Association of National Advertisers 2005 "Multicultural Excellence" award. Ron Buford, the coordinator of the "God is Still Speaking," campaign, told the *United Church News*: "The church has been given this multicultural excellence award because we didn't take the brand and make it multicultural, we took multicultural and made it a brand. This is the essence of non-conformity with the world."[27] The rhetoric and especially the logic of this statement merit careful consideration. How, for example, is "branding" of any sort an exercise in non-conformity? It is also not obvious that the UCC's effort to be "multicultural" is succeeding. The case of the Puerto Rico Conference and its subsequent departure from the UCC fold, for example, challenges this notion.

A third consequence of the campaign was the inclusion of two United Church of Christ leaders in *OUT* magazine's list of 2005's "Most Intriguing Gay Men, Lesbians, and Straight Allies." John Thomas, the denomination's General Minister and President, was listed among nine "straight allies" for his support of same-gender marriage equality. Ron Buford, who, the magazine noted, is gay, was recognized for his leadership of The Stillspeaking Initiative. The *UC News* quoted *OUT* magazine's praise for Buford and the denomination: "While many denominations are spewing anti-gay venom, the United Church of Christ created TV spots that trumpeted acceptance and welcome of gays. After CBS and NBC refused to show the commercials, Buford exposed their censorship and raised even more money for time on cable TV."[28]

PART THREE: THE CONTROVERSIAL AND WHIMSICAL AD CAMPAIGN CONTINUES

In the heady environment that ensued after the media response to the first ads, the "God is Still Speaking" campaign undertook a second ad campaign scheduled to begin during the Advent season of 2005. Whereas the first commercials were financed in large part by one-time loans or donations from various agencies of the UCC, the second round of ads sought direct financial support from the UCC's 5,000-plus congregations, especially the 2,300 or so that had "opted-in" to the TSI program. "It's going to be edgy again and it's going to create buzz," Ron Buford said concerning the second coming of the advertising campaign. Only "one small thing" was holding up the appearance of the new ad, namely $3 million.[29] In a speech delivered in Atlanta, Ron Buford appealed to the General Synod XXV for support in the amount of $1.5 million. He announced that the UCC's Collegium of Officers had agreed to approach the UCC's four national Covenanted Ministries—Local Church Ministries, Wider Church Ministries, Justice and Witness Ministries, and the Office of General Ministries—with a request that they collectively match the $1.5 million figure if the churches could raise the same sum by November 1st or "All Saints Day." "Between now and October, it is not a lot to ask these churches for," Buford said; he added that enthusiasts had told him: "yes, this is something that we want to do" and "yes, this is something that we can do."[30]

But despite the publicity surrounding the denomination and the notoriety that ensued after the "Bouncer Ad" controversy, the denomination was unable to elicit sufficient funds from its churches to begin a second round of provocative TV ads during the Christmas season in 2005. Writing an open letter to the "Stillspeaking Friends," Ron Buford announced on November 7th that "the Advent buy is off." While presumably not commenting on the churches' collective failure to support the campaign with additional finances (the extraordinary demand for giving in the aftermath of earthquakes and hurricanes during the spring and summer of the year were noted as causes), Buford asserted "Our campaign slogan is more than a slogan; it is God's promise: God is still speaking,".[31] Buford went on to promise that the needed funds would be accounted for by the spring and that the ad campaign would continue during the season of Lent 2006.

Although lack of funding delayed the appearance of the follow-up ad for a season, the "Ejector Pew" ad did come to public attention, finally, at the end of March 2006. The message and the strategy of the "God is Still Speaking," campaign continued: once again the ad was banned by the major networks; once again the ad's rejection occurred well in advance of the anticipated air date; and once again the UCC's Office of Communication orchestrated a response to the ban, beginning with the suggestion of a conspiracy to undermine the campaign a week prior to its official debut.[32] Embraced by the campaign's leaders, various focus groups, and a number of the denomination's national agencies, conferences, and congregations, the continuation of the campaign "received significant response" (as well as criticism) within and outside the denomination.[33]

The "Ejector Pew" Ad

At a press conference in Cleveland on March 27, 2006, UCC church leaders unveiled the new national TV ad. It begins with the sound of a vaguely baroque melody reverberating from a church organ. The opening shot reveals a large sanctuary as viewed from the chancel. The voice of a crying baby can be heard, at first as if in the distance. The cries become louder as the camera zooms in on a smug-looking white middle class family of three; they pass before a large, traditional stained glass window on their way to taking their seats in a pew near the middle of the sanctuary. An African American woman, seated near the white family, struggles uneasily to silence the baby she is holding in her arms even while the baby's cries become louder. The patriarch of the white family looks over at the African American woman with disdain. An old, wrinkled hand appears on the screen; its thumb presses a red button; and all of a sudden the African American woman is ejected from her pew and hurled into the air. Next a young man places his arm around the young man next to him as if to settle in; but that thumb appears again to press another button and the two go flying up in the air. Then a gentleman, Arab in appearance, looks about somewhat nervously; the thumb appears again and he is thrust by a huge springboard from his seat. The thumb presses more buttons; more people are ejected; the organ meanders on oblivious to the drama that is unfolding all around. Eventually, a differently-abled person flips in the air (with another stained glass window in the background), cries out, and drops his walker. Finally, a woman looking very much like the stereotypical homeless person (large overcoat, wool-knit cap) takes a seat near the patriarchal white male; he, his wife, and his daughter slide away from her and down the pew in anticipation of the rejection that is about to come.

The music switches to an acoustic guitar strummed in a manner and a tone resembling George Harrison on the Beatles' song "Here Comes the Sun." The screen fades to black. Then, in white lettering, the words appear: "God doesn't reject people"; and "Neither do we." A multitude of smiling faces appears on the screen as the voice-over announces: "The United Church of Christ: No matter who you are or where you are on life's journey, you're welcome here." Close-ups of individual faces from the congregation flash onto the screen (elderly people; young people; black, white, and yellow people; men and women; boys and girls). Drums kick up a happy beat and the UCC logo, in white, appears on a field of red. Underneath the denomination's name, in black, is the slogan "God is still speaking," and below that is the denomination's web site address.

Media Response to the Ad and the Response to the Media Response

The major networks responded to the UCC's second ad in much the same manner as with the first. In a memo sent in August 2005 (four months before the anticipated ad run in December and over six months prior to the official release of the commercial), ABC referred to the network's longstanding policy precluding approval of commercials that made reference to "religious doctrine and/or religious themes." Perhaps whimsically, the memo made the following stipulation in capital letters: "PLEASE ENSURE THAT IT IS CLEAR THAT NO ONE IS INJURED AFTER BEING EJECTED FROM THE PEWS."[34] Of course the denomination's point, it might be argued, was that people were in fact injured, seriously and sometimes physically, after experiencing some form of rejection in church. CBS interpreted the ad as "advocacy advertising," with no further specifics.[35] NBC initially rejected the ad because it presented "views on controversial issues." Asked to review the policy, the vice president of advertising standards reconsidered the ad, rejected it again for the same reason, and offered to review "any revisions [the UCC may] wish to submit."[36]

Shortly after the resounding rejection of the ad by the major networks, Ron Buford met with high-level CBS executives. According to his account in an open letter to friends of the Stillspeaking campaign, Buford asked of CBS: "What has to change for the United Church of Christ ad to be acceptable, to not be considered an 'advocacy ad'?" A CBS executive allegedly replied that "it would have to become commonplace across the U.S. for churches to welcome gays and lesbians."[37] Many in the UCC could be expected to find this kind of stipulation disturbing. The denomination's twenty-fifth General Synod, meeting in Atlanta on July 4, 2005, had passed a resolution in support of equal marriage rights for all, regardless of gender. The resolution also called upon congregations to adopt wedding policies that did not discriminate against gay or lesbian couples.[38] In the controversies leading up to the appearance of the "Ejector Pew" ad on cable—but not network—television, a CBS spokesperson was queried concerning the network's definition of "controversial." With reference to Ron Buford's account of their conversation about the "Ejector Pew" as an advocacy ad, Shannon Jacobs said: "That supposed exchange is simply fictitious."[39]

Meanwhile, the denomination stirred up internal controversy about the ad just prior to its release. In an article entitled "Details of UCC's new TV ad emerge earlier than planned," J. Bennett Guess wrote that *ucctruths.com*, "a website known for its negative critiques of the UCC's National and Conference settings," had published a description of the ad a week before its anticipated release on March 27, 2006. The article criticized *ucctruths.com*'s use of a still photograph depicting a man from the advertisement separated from his walker and flying in the air—the same incident that so exercised ABC with reference to the potential injury caused to the actor involved. Diverging from earlier defenses of the ad campaign's overall whimsical approach, the article quoted David Denham, a minister in the UCC's Disabilities Ministries, who lamented: "I have been deeply aware of such a possibility of disability being used as a wedge issue." The article went on to criticize the *ucctruths.org*'s website, saying it was "long-known to lambaste UCC leaders." The article did concede, however, that the ad had been previewed in a number of venues including *Sojourners Magazine* and the UCC's New England Women's Gathering.[40]

The Air of Controversy During the Second Ad Campaign

The period before and after the second ad's appearance was one of great controversy within the United Church of Christ. Apart from the denomination's continuing financial difficulties, the ad appeared in the immediate aftermath of the "Marriage Equality" resolution of General Synod XXV. The ideology of the ad insists that "no matter who you are or where you are on life's journey, you're welcome here." Some embraced this message before and after the "Ejector Pew" ad and some have measured the rhetoric and found it lacking in substance. Examples of victory and strife abound.

Shortly after General Synod XXV, the Southern Conference of the United Church of Christ circulated a letter under the heading "Whether Disturbed or Excited, Continue the Dialogue."[41] The letter describes in brief detail how the "Marriage Equality for All" resolution came into being. It then veers into a discussion about "a present and sinister threat" in the Conference, a "fox in the henhouse that is seeking to steal our most vulnerable churches." The reference is to the "Evangelical Association of Reformed and Congregational Christian Churches" or "EA," a group of UCC persons who, according to the Southern Conference writers, "are intent on causing havoc in local churches and sow division within [the] Conferences." In boldface, the letter declares: ". . . **any church that is affiliated with the Evangelical Association is no longer seeking to be in good standing or in covenant with the United Church of Christ or the Southern Conference**." Resorting to rhetoric of an earlier era, the letter draws toward its closing with a reference to the activities of the Evangelical Association as "outside agitation."

The situation as represented by members of the Evangelical Association differs in many respects from the characterization contained in the Southern Conference's letter.[42] On one point, however, both groups do agree: that participation in the Evangelical Association is grounds for dismissal from the United Church of Christ. This fact is worth pondering in relation to The Stillspeaking Initiative's rhetoric of extravagant welcome.

The irony of the situation was not remarked upon by the John Thomas, the denomination's General Minister and President. In an uncharacteristically polemical report delivered to the UCC's Executive Council in October 2005, Thomas claimed that the Evangelical Association along with another "renewal" group in the UCC, the Biblical Witness Fellowship, entertained a "long-term agenda of silencing a progressive voice while enlisting the church in an unholy alliance with right wing politics." Although no evidence is cited for this claim, Thomas goes on to characterize the situation in rhetoric typical of the current era: "we doves innocently entertain these serpents in our midst at our own peril."[43] Ideology to the contrary, apparently there are some who "are **not** welcome here."

Two weeks after Thomas's address to the Executive Council, a great welcome was anticipated. As mentioned previously, the Dallas, Texas-based Cathedral of Hope voted to join the UCC. The Rev. Jo Hudson, the church's senior pastor and rector, praised the UCC for "becoming the first mainstream denomination to support marriage rights for same gender couples." The UCC's values "are our values," Hudson said; "and we look forward to joining in partnership and continuing the work for which God has called us together." Placing this affiliation in a wider context, the article noted that in addition to the 4,300 member Cathedral of Hope, two other large-membership churches were considering the possibility of joining the UCC. One of these, the 2,000 member Plymouth Congregational Church in Minneapolis, had been part of a group of churches that resisted the United Church of Christ union in 1957 under the direction of its pastor, Howard Conn. The other, the Higher Dimensions Family Church in Tulsa, Oklahoma, was a mega-church founded by the Oral Roberts Evangelistic Ministries in 1985.[44] If not **all** are welcome in the UCC, the diversity represented by this collection of churches certainly suggests that many indeed are welcome.

Two further consequences are worthy of note. On June 7, 2006, Ron Buford left the directorship of The Stillspeaking Initiative to assume a position as consultant with the denomination's new "Congregational Vitality Initiative." Buford's role in TSI had been to generate entrepreneurial ideas. According to the UCC's online news service, Buford had perceived after joining the national UCC staff in 2000 that the denomination suffered from a "decades-old identity crisis tied to the church's dynamic-yet-confused heritage" in the aftermath of the 1957 merger. Buford understood that the "UCC lacked a 'brand'"; consequently, he argued that "the church members' pride in their denomination was being held back by an ineffective articulation of the church's history and cultural contributions." Into this lamentable milieu, Buford inserted the comma. And so, the article suggests, the "God is Still Speaking," campaign's "Bouncer Ad" and "Ejector Pew" ad "became known nationally for their edgy, youthful appeal and won several prestigious advertising awards for their multicultural and gay-affirming messages." Having accomplished his mission, the article seems to suggest, the time was right for others to pick up where Buford left off.[45]

A second consequence—not of the ad campaign itself but perhaps in response to the controversial viewpoint that the ads advanced—was the vote by the UCC's Puerto Rico Conference on June 13, 2006, to sever its ties with the denomination. According to the denominational news service, the *Iglesia Evangelica Unida de Puerto Rico* voted to disaffiliate "because of discomfort over the UCC's stance on lesbian, gay, bisexual and transgender issues."[46] In this particular instance, it appears, the UCC's multicultural agenda and its lesbian, gay, bi-sexual, and transgender-affirming agenda conflicted.

CONCLUSION: THE CAMPAIGN FOR IDENTITY AND IDENTIFICATION

In a letter dated April 2006 and addressed to conferences and congregations of the United Church of Christ, John Thomas reflected on the reception of the "Ejector Pew" ad. Seemingly perplexed, Thomas noted that while the ad was received favorably by the denomination's ecumenical partners, intense concern about the ad's message was registered by "a number of... UCC pastors and members." As with the first commercial, Thomas remarks in his second paragraph, "the primary audience [for the 'Ejector Pew' ad] is persons who do not belong to any church, not our own members." Why a negative reaction to the ad arises among UCC members and not among unchurched people or the denomination's ecumenical partners is an issue whose implications Thomas expresses the hope to explore further "over the next few months," presumably in conversation with the broader church.[47]

As a kind of conclusion to the narrative constructed here and as a preliminary and tentative response to the invitation for more discussion, I'd like to suggest that the crux of the problem signaled by The Stillspeaking Initiative lies in the gap between the churched and the unchurched; or, to characterize the gap slightly differently: The difficulty lies in the distinction between the targeted audience of the commercials and the targeted financers of the commercials. There are many ways in which the television ads might rightfully be said to have succeeded. These include generating editorials and other media responses to the ads; the appearance of various denominational executives on the major television and radio "talk shows"; and the number of "hits" recorded on the denomination's web site. Indeed, as the commercials continue to air on the denomination's web site and places like "myspace" on the internet, there's no telling what influence the ads might ultimately exert. But if Ron Buford is correct in his assertion that "money really is the language of love," then the television advertising campaign, at least, has not been a success. For the vast majority of the UCC's churches, including the vast majority of those churches that "opted-in" to the campaign, the financing of the television ads was not a priority.

Why not? Doubtless there are many answers to this question. To enter into a preliminary exploration of the question, I'd like to suggest that one approach to an answer lies in the ads themselves. While it is true that both ads are edgy, whimsical, and to a degree humorous, they place UCC loyalists in a difficult position for at least three reasons: the ads are critical of the very churches they endeavor to promote; the ads participate in a rhetoric less recognizably religious and more typical of the "culture wars"—particularly as they have been waged rhetorically during the current "War on Terrorism" era; and finally, the ads do not tell the truth—or at least not the whole truth.

I will use the "Ejector Pew" ad as the more benign, but nevertheless problematic, example. An obvious contrast is made in this ad between the old and the new and, by implication, the bad and the good. The old is signaled by the organ playing in the background of the first half of the ad; the new is represented by the guitar and drums that come in later. The old is the massive church building with its stained glass windows and high-arched ceilings; the new is the closely collected community gathering in a warm room for a portrait. The old is the ancient hand that pushes the button to eject people from the pews; the new is the loving hand gently placed upon a friend or partner. A problem arises because what is depicted as old and bad is also familiar. Many UCC churches look like the one portrayed in the ad. They are places of comfort for their members. So when the ad suggests that these places are discriminatory to the point of violence, UCC members are likely to assume that the ad represents an attack upon their own local congregation. And perhaps it does.

This sharp contrast between the old and new sets up a binary opposition characteristic of contemporary political rhetoric. In the culture war there is "the axis of evil" and, in contrast, the "freedom-loving people" of the rest of the world. There are those who, like the once-youthful Billy Joel, accept others "just the way you are" and there are those for whom "just the way you are" is not good enough.[48] If this kind of rhetoric is inadequate in the culture at large—as the approval ratings of the reigning President of the United States seem to suggest it is—then it is certainly not the kind of rhetoric one would expect a self-described "prophetic" church to indulge in. Besides, the slogans fall short, Christianly speaking. Jesus' first words were not "no matter where you are on life's journey, you're welcome here." They were a proclamation of the approaching reign of God with an accompanying call for repentance.[49] What humanity needs to repent from is a large debate within the UCC, ranging, for example, from homophobia at one end of the spectrum, to homosexuality at the other. The point is: The real church, the one the members know, is more a debating society when it comes to matters of deep conviction and less an outcropping of the "welcome wagon" enterprise.

Finally, the "Ejector Pew" is not entirely truthful in its construction of the UCC myth. Even while new, large, and independent churches have been attracted to the idea that "you are welcome here," other churches with deep ties to the denomination have left the fold. The Puerto Rico Conference's departure from the denomination offers a striking parable that cuts to the heart of the UCC's multicultural mythology. Meanwhile, other groups whose alliances lean to the right politically and theologically are openly castigated by conference ministers and other leaders of the denomination. Such admonition may come as a necessary product of church leadership; nevertheless, when it comes, it exposes as a lie the rhetorical claim of welcome to all regardless of "who you are or where you are on life's journey."

The "God is Still Speaking," television campaign was successful inasmuch as it made identification of the denomination and some of its priorities possible for millions of Americans. But as an identity campaign, as a campaign to instruct current members of the denomination in the common bonds that hold individuals and churches together in community (what the Congregationalists of an earlier era called "fellowship"), the television campaign, at least, created more difficulties than it solved. Indeed, it helped instigate, for some, a crisis of identity. And for this reason, I suspect, many UCC members neither viewed the ads with "increasing enthusiasm," nor did they place a comma instead of a period on the checks they sent in to the denomination.

NOTES

I would like to express my gratitude to the Louisville Institute for the Study of Religion in America. The award of a "Religious Institutions Grant" for the academic year 2005-2006 made possible my research into the Stillspeaking campaign.

1. Ron Buford and Randy Varcho, "Playing Catch with God," *New Conversations* (Winter, 2004), 63-67.
2. *Ibid.*, 63.
3. Deathbed, or near-deathbed, communiqués bear a certain weight in the United Church of Christ. Shortly before his death, according to one written account, Robert Moss, president of the denomination, composed an inclusive version of the UCC's *Statement of Faith* which he offered to the churches as a sort of farewell gift. According to an alternative oral tradition, the "Moss

Version" of the *Statement* was discovered among the papers in Moss's desk after his death and was circulated as a final tribute to his leadership. See Frederick R. Trost and Barbara Brown Zikmund, eds., *The Living Theological Heritage of the United Church of Christ*, Volume 7 (Cleveland: Pilgrim Press, 2005), 33-35.

4. Buford and Varcho,*Op. cit.*, 64.
5. For example, the humor inherent in the "Ejector Seat" ad. This reading of the Buford and Varcho account does not mean to suggest that Buford or Varcho were or are Pentecostal Christians, or that the meanings conjured up here were intended by the authors.
6. For a critical theological reading of the Buford and Varcho account, see James L. Haddix, "And the Word of God Came to Jonah a Second Time," *Prism* , Vol. 19, Number 2 (Fall, 2004), 41-58; see, in particular, 47-52.
7. George Rawson (1807-1899) altered, "We Limit not the Truth of God" in *The New Century Hymnal* (Cleveland: Pilgrim, 1995), 136. The original wording, not a wish but an affirmation, reads: "The Lord hath yet more light and truth to break forth from his Word." Compare "We Limit not the Truth of God" in *The Pilgrim Hymnal* (Boston: Pilgrim, 1958), 259.
8. Buford and Varcho, *Op. cit.*, 64. Mr. Varcho "cringes when told this" (that he is a "design genius") according to the text; apparently, as co-author of this article, he does not cringe with the retelling.
9. *Ibid.*, 65. The "ecstatic" quality of the experience, again a characteristic of Pentecostalism, receives emphasis here.
10. *Ibid.*, 67. The use of optimistic adjectives to suggest the popularity and success of the campaign is worthy of closer scrutiny.
11. Unitarian Universalist pastor and historian, Scott Axford remarks [in personal correspondence]: "The earliest citation [of Robinson's words] is in Edward Winslow's 1648 work, *Hypocrisy Unmasked*, in which he bewails Lutheran and hyper-Calvinist rigidities among other things. The much-remembered words, which are part of a longer sentence, are: '...the Lord has more truth and light yet to break forth out of his holy word.' While we have no text from Robinson himself, this is the recollection of someone who heard the farewell sermon based on Ezra 8:21." For the purposes of theological reflection in historical continuity with Robinson, it is worth noting that the referent—as would be expected of a 17th century Puritan—is to Scripture and not, for example, to the charismatic experience of an individual "saint."
12. Buford and Varcho, *Op. cit.*, 65.
13. *Ibid.*
14. Henry T. Blackaby, *Experiencing God* (Nashville: Broadman and Holman, 1994),36. See the unpublished essay by Joseph David Stinson, "A Comma and a Period: Searching for the Theological Underpinning for a Slogan," a paper presented to the New Jersey Association of the Central Atlantic Conference, March 20, 2003.
15. J. Bennett Guess, "Church Leaders Agree: Financial Troubles Demand a United Effort." http:www.ucc.org/uccnews/nov03/struggles.html.
16. Quoted in Guess, "Church Leaders Agree."

17. J. Bennett Guess, "'Catalyst Project' Seeks to Inspire Increased Giving to Local Churches," *United Church News* Volume 20, Number 1 (January/February, 2004), 8. Also available at http://www.ucc.org/ucnews/feb04/catalyst.htm.
18. A portion of this discussion is derived from Theodore Louis Trost, "The Passion and the Compassion of the Christ," in Scott Paeth, ed., *Who Do You Say That I Am? Christology and Identity in the United Church of Christ* (Cleveland: United Church Press, 2005), 151-152.
19. Memo from Robert L. Lowary (CBS) to Ms. Jena Stadtlander, February 19, 2004.
20. J. Bennett Guess, "Welcome to the Show," http://www.ucc.org/ucnews/mar04/welcome.htm.
21. See, for example, J. Bennett Guess, "National Ad Campaign Hinges on UCC Members' Financial Support," *United Church News*, October 2004. There is no reference to the "rejected" status of the national ad in this article.
22. See J. Bennett Guess, "On the Air," *United Church News*, November 2004.
23. See http://www.stillspeaking.com/news/releases.html.
24. See http://stillspeaking.com/news/release2.html. This contrast between program content and advertising content received significant emphasis in the coming year as efforts continued to have the UCC's ads aired. It is worth wondering, at least in passing, why the denomination would want to advertise on networks whose programs it so disparages.
25. See Administrator, "Only recently did UCC learn of networks' ultimate refusal of church ads," December 2, 2004, http://news.ucc.org/.
26. "Dallas' Cathedral of Hope, amid [sic] others, Seeks UCC affiliation," *United Church News*, Volume 21, Number 6 (December/January, 2006), 3.
27. J. Bennett Guess, "Stillspeaking's 'Bouncer' Receives 'Biggie' Advertising Award," November 11, 2005, http://news.ucc.org/.
28. J. Bennett Guess, "Two UCC Leaders Honored Among OUT Magazine's Top 100 List," November 15, 2005, http://news.ucc.org/.
29. Will C. Matthews, "New Commercial Planned for Advent," September 5, 2005, http://www.ucc.org/ucnews/sep05/advent.htm.
30. *Ibid.*
31. Buford, "The Day After. . . " November 2, 2005, http://www.stillspeaking.com/news/rb110705.html.
32. J. Bennett Guess, "Details of UCC's new TV ad emerge earlier than planned," March 21, 2006, http://news.ucc.org/.
33. John H. Thomas, "Reflections on 'Ejector': United Church of Christ Television Commercial," April, 2006.
34. Memo from Stacy B Jacob (ABC) to Lisa Kalmus (Gotham Advertising Agency), August 8, 2005.
35. Memo from Autumn Polansky (CBS) to Lisa Kalmus, August 5, 2005.
36. Memo from Dorothy Busz (NBC) to Lisa Kalmus, August 5, 2005; letter from Victoria Morgan to Lisa Kalmus, September 30, 2005.
37. Ron Buford, "We Will not be Silenced," October 20, 2006, http://www.

stillspeaking.com/news/releases.html.

38. See the summary of the resolution in "Synod Scorecard," *United Church News* Volume 21, Number 4 (August/September, 2005), A13.

39. "UCC's Buford Called out by CBS," from a story in the *Knoxville* [Tennessee] *News Sentinel*, March 28, 2006, quoted in http://ucctruths.com/Archive/2006MarchArchive.html.

40. J. Bennett Guess, "Details of UCC's new TV ad emerge earlier than planned," http:www.ucc.org/uccnews/.

41. Stephen W. Camp, et al, "Whether Disturbed or Excited, Continue the Dialogue," July, 2005.

42. Personal correspondence between the author and two Evangelical Association ministers.

43. Quoted in J. Bennett Guess, "Prodigal's Resentful 'Older Brother' Still Undermines Faithfulness," October 15, 2005, http://news.ucc.org/. See also "John Thomas, 'The Older Brother in our Midst': Report to UCC Executive Council," October 14, 2005.

44. J. Bennett Guess, "Cathedral of Hope Votes Overwhelmingly to Join UCC," November 1, 2005, http://news.ucc.org/. For a description of Howard Conn's critique of the proposed merger and the vehemence with which the Plymouth Congregational Church originally resisted the merger, see Theodore Louis Trost, *Douglas Horton and the Ecumenical Impulse in American Religion* (Cambridge: Harvard University Press, 2002), 83-96.

45. Administrator, "Buford, Architect of UCC's 'Stillspeaking' Campaign, to Assume New Role," June 7, 2006, http://news.ucc.org.

46. Barb Powell, "Vote by UCC Puerto Rico Conference to disaffiliate 'deeply painful,' says UCC leader," June 13, 2006, http://news.ucc.org.

47. John H. Thomas, "Reflections on 'Ejector.'"

48. Billy Joel, "Just the Way You Are," *The Stranger* (Columbia Records, 1977).

49. After he emerges from his forty day sojourn in the wilderness, Jesus declares: "The time is fulfilled and the kingdom of God has come near. Repent and believe in the good news!" (Mark 1.15 NRSV).

THE EMBODIED SEMINARY

Reflections on Holistic Theological Education

Bruce Epperly

I.

The seminary has often viewed itself as the "mind" of the church. Within its cloistered walls, tradition is preserved, reflection nurtured, and new forms of practice explored whose impact radiates across the wider body of the church through the influence of seminary graduates, lay students, lectures and consultations, and faculty publications. It is no surprise that seminaries often have seen their relationship to the church as unilateral. The role of the seminary is to provide resources and training for the church, while it receives little from congregations and judicatories in terms of what truly matters to the seminary's vocation. While the church is the laboratory and source of students for seminary programs, seminary communities often aspire to stay above the fray of the congregational and denominational politics, membership statistics, demographics, and social changes that are a matter of life and death for mainstream and progressive Christianity today.

Today, the image of the seminary as the mind of the church needs to be transformed in light of new understandings of mind-body and creature-environment relationships described by medicine, biology, physics, ecology, and post-modern theology.' While each of these fields has its own unique perspective on the mind-body relationship, they share a common vision

Bruce Epperly is Director of Continuing Education and Associate Professor of Practical Theology at Lancaster Theological Seminary, and is co-pastor of Disciples United Church of Christ in Lancaster.

of reality and human existence as a lively and intricate web of relatedness, characterized by continuity rather than discontinuity, in which multiple centers of value, experience, and interpretation constantly interact with and shape one another.

In light of the growing vision of microcosmic and macrocosmic relatedness described by quantum physics and mind-body medicine, we can affirm that the mind is embodied and the body is inspired. This insight suggests a lively, relational, embodied vision of human life in which the mind is shaped by the body, and the body, conversely, is constantly transformed by our thoughts and emotions. From this perspective, the image of the seminary as the mind of the church describes a lively, dynamic, symbiotic relationship of constant give and take in which the well-being of the seminary and church are intimately related.

It is clear that the "body" of mainstream Protestantism is seriously diseased. While certain individual cells or organs are flourishing, the body of the church–as seen in terms of denominational health and overall congregational vitality–is at a "tipping point" in which the full recovery or even survival of the patient is in doubt. It is clear that the health of the mainstream Protestantism has radically shaped–and will continue to shape–the health of seminaries in terms of finances, enrollment, and morale. Today, seminaries can no longer depend on denominational and congregational bodies for financial support and consistent enrollment, but must seek nourishment in the few financially healthy cells remaining. But, the well-being of these cells and their ability–and desire–to provide adequate nourishment to the "mind" is jeopardized by the critical condition of mainstream Protestantism.

The philosopher Alfred North Whitehead describes three ways that organisms respond to significant changes in their environment: 1) denial of the threat, 2) chaotic disruption, or the internal acquiescence to external realities, and 3) the origination of novelty to match the novelty of the environment.[3] These can be roughly identified with the pattern of response to life-threats articulated by thanatologist Elizabeth Kubler-Ross. While congregations and seminaries have, for the most part, been forced to abandon the path of denial in light of the concrete reality of statistics and long-term prospects for institutional viability, they find themselves somewhere between 1) hopelessly and passively surrendering to inevitable decline, powerlessness, and irrelevance and 2) initiating novelty to match the radical political, cultural, and demographic changes of our time.[4]

If it is to continue to be the mind of the church, even a diseased church, the role of the seminary is clear and challenging–to be a conscious and intentional partner with congregations, denominations, emerging configurations of faith communities, and lay and professional Christian leaders in facilitating creative transformation and initiating novelty to match the novelty of the current cultural and congregational environment. The seminary as the mind of the church is called to do what the mind does best–envisage possibilities and explore new practices in relationship to the concrete realities of the church and world.

The seminary's vocation is to be a bearer of health to the encompassing body. But, in line with the image of the mind, the seminary must also "embody" these possibilities and practices in light of the congregational body which is both its environmental companion and source of nourishment. Apart from the experiential wisdom and nourishment of the body–even the "sick" bodies of contemporary mainstream Protestantism–the seminary will become disembodied, irrelevant, and ultimately incapacitated.

Still, if the current medical images of mind-body interdependence relate to human interactions at the macro as well as the micro level, then the creativity and concreteness of the embodied seminary will be the source of ideas, images, practices, and possibilities that add vitality to the experiences of congregations, laypersons, and professional Christian leaders, and may become the tipping point from death to life and toward the eventual future flourishing of new forms of mainstream and progressive Christianity. Still, we must never forget that there is no ultimate dividing line between mind and body and that the mind's own well-being depends on the health of the surrounding environment of cells and the body as a whole.

The seminary cannot afford to be ideologically or practically isolated from the church, nor can the seminary compartmentalize and objectify its relationships to congregations or judicatories. In a relational world, there is no "other." Paul's image of the body of Christ serves to inspire health in congregations as well as seminary-church relationships. When one member succeeds, all succeed. When one is diseased, all are at risk. (I Corinthians 12).

In the following paragraphs, I will suggest a vision and practice for an embodied seminary that is dynamically related to congregations and denominations as sources of inspiration and recipients of insights. Holistic in its understanding of theological education, the embodied seminary recognizes that its greatest gifts to church and society will be 1) the theological and professional liveliness, innovation, and well-being of its graduates and lay participants and 2) its commitment to creative and life-supporting interdependence with church and culture.'

II.

Interdependence and theological education. In the Western medical tradition, two aims of health care have been prominent–preventative and reactive/restorative medicine. Preventative medicine traditionally refers to the practices of wholeness–diet, exercise, environment, spiritual formation, mindfulness, sabbath keeping, stress reduction, and healthy relationships –that nurture overall well-being in persons and communities. Reactive and restorative medicine refers to life-saving or remedial responses to diseases of mind, body, and spirit through changes in lifestyle, surgery, medication, chemotherapy, and spiritual healing practices (such as meditation for stress reduction, imagination to enhance immune functioning, biofeedback, healing touch and laying on of hands). Health crises challenge both the patient and health care provider to initiate reactive responses to promote a cure and also, if there is likelihood of survival, preventative follow-up practices to ensure on-going health and wholeness.

This medical metaphor has bearing on our understanding of theological education today. As the primary source of professional training, the seminary is responsible to support congregations through training in preventative and reactive/restorative theological education. While, at first glance, both foci might fall into the realms of pastoral theology, practical theology, and church administration, in actuality, every seminary subject has a preventative and reactive/restorative component. Indeed, the biblical story and the history of Christianity might be read as a dynamic interplay of prevention, restoration, and innovation in relations among humans and in the divine-human relationship. For example, exploring the breadth of biblical scholarship or theological reflection enables future church leaders to respond creatively to theological pluralism and controversy within congregational life. Courses in church history enable pastors and congregations to gain a larger perspective on God's presence within the church and the many options in Christian practice as well as to recognize that Christian practice and theology are pluralistic, rather than monolithic, in nature. Here, the image of prevention is not meant to describe homeostasis, although this is important to both personal and institutional health, but a lively and innovative interaction with the internal and external environment that promotes a fully-functioning organism, be it a person, congregation, or denomination.

Current research in medical practice, professional relationships, and complementary health care focuses on the interdependence of mind and body, person and environment, professional and patient, and spirituality and health. Dynamic visions of health affirm that 1) wholeness embraces the totality of a person's life; 2) spiritual, intellectual, and physical well-being are intimately connected; and 3) physicians and other professionals depend on the trust and respect of the communities they serve. This same interdependence also applies to theological education–seminaries arise from and contribute to congregations and denominations; creative theological ideas are tested in congregational and professional settings; seminary well-being depends on the trust given by congregations and judicatory officials; demographic and theological trends in denominations shape seminary enrollments; and popular culture influences the foci of theological education, implicitly, if not explicitly.[6] At the very least, these influences challenge the seminary to be lively, agile, and creative in responding to popular trends in theological reflection as well as controversial issues in the church.[7] Seminaries need to initiate novelty in curriculum, practice, and professional education in order to match the novelty of the broader church and secular culture.

The seminary's role in preventing disease and promoting health in the wider church challenges the seminary community to anticipate the needs of pastors and congregations. The seminary's role in responding to illness in the church requires the seminary to take what is already happening in congregations and professional ministry seriously and provide novel and non-defensive responses to areas of congregational and professional disease. Seminary courses and training events need to be futuristic as well as historical in their orientation.

Imagination and adventure. Walter Brueggemann has spoken of the prophetic task as that of envisaging alternatives to the present unjust–and diseased–social situation. In light of an embodied and futuristic approach to theological education, seminaries are challenged to envisage the possibilities, both positive and negative, emerging from our current situation. Whether or not we accept it, we are on an adventure into uncharted educational, spiritual, and congregational frontiers. Our task is to make this pilgrimage a "holy adventure," that is, one in which we can creatively respond to–and anticipate–change in ways that deepen the faith of pastors and their congregations. Our calling is to ponder what the next step of congregational and professional life will be, and adapt our educational approaches to help guide pilgrims on their way. To support the health of pastors and congregations, we must be willing to be institutionally and academically lively and agile. Without abandoning marginal congregations, we must–again, in light of the mind-body metaphor–identify healthy, imaginative, and vital congregations and church leaders, and nurture their growth not only to strengthen their health but to tip the balance toward health in congregations, associations, regions, and denominations. These are the "organs" and "cells" vital to the survival of the larger body as well as the mind.[8]

Concrete theology. If the image of mind-body relatedness is accurate both medically and theologically, then everything that happens in the mind influences the body, and vice versa. Seminaries shape congregations through the focus of the curriculum and the theological orientation of the community and faculty. Congregations and lay and professional church leaders shape seminaries through the values of the students, the pressing issues of congregational and denominational life and decision-making, and their own personal health and well-being. Accordingly, every seminary class and worship service arises from and radiates into the larger world of the church.

This metaphysical and biblical vision of relatedness constantly reminds the seminary that it ultimately deals in concrete theological and professional situations and not intellectual abstractions. The unavoidable concreteness of theological education calls us to be mindful about the impact of our curriculum, focus, and methodology on the broader theological and congregational environment. Seminary faculty and administration must ask the following questions: Do our classes contribute to the well-being and vitality of pastors and congregations? Do they provide guidance for the practice of ministry and church leadership? Do they explicitly take into account the real as well as ideal church? Is the "mind" of the church providing the "body" with adequate spiritual, theological, and professional nourishment for the challenges of the day? Do our courses provide practical guidance for conveying theological education to lay persons? And, perhaps, most significantly, are we truly listening to the church that depends on our guidance?

Healthy ministry. Although there is great pathology within the church today, we must place the health and well-being of pastors and lay and professional church leaders at the center of the curriculum and not at its periphery. The primary tool of ministry is the pastor's and congregational leader's ability to respond to the stresses of a constantly changing ministry as well as to provide wisdom and creativity for a frontier church. Nurturing healthy ministry is primarily preventative in nature, since many of the most difficult challenges of church life are matters of health, communication, and wise decision-making.

Courses in professional wellness, stress reduction, and spiritual formation should be integral to seminary curricula and field education along with courses related to the arts of ministry, ministry in a post-modem age, mission, transformational leadership, holistic stewardship, and church leadership.[9] Greater emphasis should be given in seminary classes to the professional and spiritual implications of the respective theological disciplines.

Gratitude. Finally, the health of congregations and seminaries alike depends on a renewal of the practice of thanksgiving. Gratitude is the virtue of connectedness that reminds us that we are all in this together. Within the body of Christ, seminaries receive nurture from congregations in terms of students, pastor preceptors, mentors, and denominational counsel. The seminary's vocation involves partnerships with these disparate, but necessary, companions in our work. As seminaries seek to inspire congregations and denominations to greater intellectual, practical, and professional health, they are most effective when they look for what is best in each congregational or denominational setting, thank God for its presence, and choose to be partners in enhancing the good and godly work we witness. In partnerships with congregations and judicatories that are aimed at prevention, restoration, transformation, and inspiration, the seminary will live out its goal as the mind of the church.

NOTES

1. The following texts by physicians and scientists describe this new vision of the universe and human life: David Bohm, *Wholeness and the Implicate Order* (London: Rutledge, 2002); Fritjof Capra, *The Tao of Physics* (New York: Bantam Books, 1977); Larry Dossey, *Healing Words* (San Francisco: Harper San Francisco, 1994); Candace Pert, *Molecules of Emotion* (New York: Scribers, 1999); Michael Talbot, *The Holographic Universe* (New York: Harper, 1992).
2. There is nothing new in using mind-body analogies within Christianity. The Apostle Paul's image of the body of Christ suggests that Christ is the "mind" of the church body, and that we as Christ's followers are called to experience that same "mind of Christ" in our own spiritual formation.
3. For a description of responses to change see Bruce Epperly, *At the Edges of Life* (St. Louis: Chalice Press, 1992), 32-40.
4. The most creative attempts at creative transformation within the church, from my perspective, are those categorized by terms such as the "intentional congregation," (Diana Butler Bass) "emergent church," (Brian McLaren) and "ancient-future" church (Robert Webber) as well as the broad spectrum, justice-oriented visions, articulated by Jim Wallis in *God's Politics.* If it is articulated in terms of spiritual formation and theology as well as social transformation and extravagant welcome, the "God is still speaking campaign" of the UCC is also a creative attempt at congregational and denominational transformation.
5. My own vision shares much with other recent reflections on theological education such as Edward Farley's affirmation of the unity of habitus and practice in theological education; David Kelsey's recognition of the seminary's interdependence with the church and culture and call for the interplay of paideia, spiritual formation, and professional education; Rebecca Chopp's feminist theological vision of embodiment; and John Cobb and Joe Hough's focus on the seminary as a place of vocation. Each of these visions affirms the importance of context and spiritual formation as essential to training in the practice of ministry and in theological reflection.
6. Current examples of this include the UCC General Synod's pronouncement on the multiple tracks to ordination; the popularity of texts such as Rick Warren's *The Purpose Driven Life* and seminars on *Forty Days of Purpose,* the latter of which competes with seminary based lay education programs.
7. Sadly, practice has often been seen as a lesser vocation in the seminary ethos. Few, popularly-written and lay-accessible spiritual growth, biblical study, and theological "workbooks" or "devotional manuals" have come from

seminary faculty, despite the fact that evangelical and new age books (*The Prayer of Jabez, The Purpose Driven Life, Left Behind. Celestine Prophecy, The Seat of the Soul*) outsell mainstream theological and spiritual formation texts, find their way to the bestseller list, and are more likely to be read in mainstream congregations than books by mainstream and progressive theologians. The exception to this, on a smaller scale, are books by Marcus Borg, John Dominic Crossan, and John Shelby Spong.

8. At Lancaster Theological Seminary, we are strengthening current and future pastoral leadership through the Leadership Now program for high school students, Alliance for the Renewal of Ministry program for experienced pastors, the Wholeness in Ministry program for recent seminary graduates in their first congregational call, and the recently initiated Harvesting Wisdom program for pastors on the verge of retirement or recently retired.

9. The new Wholeness in Ministry Program for New Pastors at Lancaster Theological Seminary has the potential not only of supporting pastors in the their first call but serving as a feedback to the seminary in terms of its curricular and formation programs. Our hope is that listening to new pastors will guide us in our adventures in creative transformation and curricular renewal.

GENERAL SYNOD 25 AND AUTHORIZATION FOR MINISTRY

William Imes

When the history of General Synod 25 is written, it will be interesting to see which action of that Synod is regarded as the most important. Clearly for the press, the vote to affirm same-sex marriage garnered a great deal of attention. Secondary attention was paid to the resolution regarding Israel and the suggested divestment from firms doing business with Israel as a protest against the building of the wall and other actions of that nation. Over time it may well be that the pronouncement on ministerial issues proves to be the most significant action of that Synod. A pronouncement which addresses issues regarding authorization for ministry and in a tangential way the placement system itself is dealing with one of the key aspects of the common life of the United Church of Christ. It is not clear precisely how this pronouncement will affect authorization, let alone how well the changes will affect the placement system. Rather than presenting a fully developed new system, the pronouncement offered directions in which such a system might grow without making a commitment to the particulars of such a system.

When one considers all of the issues relating to authorization for ministry and the process of placement in the United Church of Christ, we are clearly talking about a system which functions in a church culture which is system resistant. It is commonplace to argue that between the Revolutionary War and the Civil War, American Protestantism underwent Methodization. It may well be equally true that in the time since the World War II and the present that much of American religion, including not only Roman Catholicism but Judaism as well, has been Congregationalized. For the last generation,

William Imes is president of Bangor Theological Seminary in Bangor, Maine.

most of the fastest growing churches and mega churches in the United States have been independent congregations. But even more importantly within many denominations congregations see themselves as self-sufficient. So the question of the nature of the Body of Christ beyond a local congregation has little theoretical or practical content or application. This observation is meant to extend far beyond the history of the Congregational tradition in the United States.

We live in a time and place where placement is one of the few issues which ties local congregations to one another. The action taken in the 2005 Synod in Atlanta will affect every congregation in the United Church of Christ. The action is intended to address a number of issues that have arisen in the process of authorizing ministry and placing ministers. In this article a brief account will be offered of the nature of the issues addressed by the pronouncement, of the process by which the pronouncement came into being, and of the issues which lie before us as the pronouncement is actually implemented.

In a narrow sense the 2005 pronouncement is a response to a resolution adopted at General Synod 22 in 1999 in Providence. In a broader sense that resolution is the result of the conversations that have been held in various settings of the United Church of Christ for many years. Some persons would argue that these conversations have taken place almost throughout the history of the denomination, others would suggest that they have become more intense in the last 25 or so years, and yet other persons would point to very specific conversations held first in the Office of Church Life and Leadership and now by the Parish Life and Leadership Team within Local Church Ministries.

The OCLL conversations alone resulted in documents a foot deep. These conversations addressed a cluster of issues relating primarily to authorization for ministry and secondarily to the question of placement. One focus of such discussions was the theology of ordination itself. A good deal of consideration of the nature of ministry has led people to conclude that it makes no sense to have any sort of act which sets some ministers apart from other ministers. A bigger threat and equally challenging question has been why people are being ordained not in terms of the separation of laity and clergy, but in these terms: Does ordination recognize gifts found in a particular individual which are understood to be of value to the whole Body of Christ or is ordination primarily an acknowledgement of a call to an individual to a particular function within the life of the church itself? Barbara Brown Zikmund labeled the former embodiment and the latter empowerment. It is clear that the four predecessor denominations of the United Church of Christ addressed this issue in different ways and in different times in their own particular histories. In the 1960s in the United Church of Christ there was a tendency to ordain people to all sorts of ministries with little or no connection and accountability to either a congregation or a judicatory. In the last 25 years or so, the pendulum has swung in the opposite direction. The United Church of Christ has been increasingly functional in looking at ordination. Most Associations have refused to ordain anyone without a very specific call to a specific ministry. (Some places have shown some creativity in allowing for specialized ministries where accountability to a local congregation was built into the covenant of which was brought into being by the ordination.)

Alongside of the questions clustered around ordination has been an increasingly vigorous conversation about licensure for lay ministry and the possibility that service in the lay ministry coupled with some sort of regional training (on a conference-wide basis) might constitute sufficient preparation for ordination. Earlier in the 20th century, the rule of four years of college and three years of seminary was just that, a goal. But by the time of the formation of the United Church of Christ that expectation was well on its way to becoming the one and only track for ordination. One was ordained for life, but a lay minister needed to be licensed every year even when that person had 20 or 30 or more years of experience in the ministry and had accumulated a great deal of continuing education and other formational experiences but had not done so in the context of a degree program.

Is there a difference between lay ministry and ordained ministry? What does licensure say about a person and that person's call, that person's service in a particular congregation? Is it distinct from what ordination says about a person, their call and their service in a particular congregation or other ministerial setting? Even bigger issues in regard to lay ministry relate to a cluster of race, class and ethnic issues. There are also major economic issues relating to the call and training of ministers and the cost of education. The decline in mainline denominational numbers in the last 40 years and the blurring of denominational lines have all contributed to much confusion, difficulty, and clear-cut instances of bias and injustice in dealing with lay ministers.

The range of issues relating to lay ministry and lay ministerial training are incredibly broad. African American pastors have one set of experiences. They raise issues of racial discrimination, of economic disadvantage, and of the helpfulness and appropriateness of a good deal of theological training.[1]

These issues are focused in different ways by different traditions. For instance, amongst Puerto Ricans the tradition has been that one is called to ministry, actually serves in a church and then attends seminary to receive further education and training. This is a common model among Baptists of all stripes in the United States where one's call is acknowledged with ordination and then one is trained and formed for that service. This has also been true of many African American denominations. It is interesting to note that in the Baptist traditions where often the processes are heavily influenced by the pastor of the local congregation both in identifying the potential ordinand and in authorizing the ordination and in more connectional settings such as the AME Church increasingly there is an emphasis on seminary education as a prerequisite for ordination.

At the same time in the situations such as exists amongst the Marshall Islanders in the United States, most of whom grew up in a Congregational tradition at home, pastors do not come to ministry with a formal education either at the college or seminary level. The question then becomes: What is the appropriate way to provide training and formation for persons who clearly are perceived as having a call and the ability to serve within their own ethnic communities? The point has often been made by CAIM representatives that amongst Native Americans mentoring is really the preferred way to provide such training and formation for ministerial students.

A number of issues relate much more to placement and to the economic reality that many congregations within the United Church of Christ are no longer able to pay for a full-time, ordained minister. Clearly many lay ministers have been paid on a very part-time basis and treated as bi-vocational rather than as full-time pastors even if their work assumes full-time proportions. The reality of the placement system is that in parts of the United Church of Christ at this time it has a great deal of difficulty in functioning. The Southeast Conference, for instance, has one Association with no ordained clergy in it; all of the pastors are licensed lay ministers. And in the Northern Plains Conference about 40% of those serving churches are now licensed lay ministers. David Moyer noted that in the early 90s when he began as the Associate Conference Minister in Wisconsin for the northern area of the state, that of the roughly 60 churches he worked with in placement, all but a handful were able to call full-time, ordained ministers either by themselves or in parishes whereas when he left that position ten years later to become Conference Minister for Wisconsin, only half of those churches were still able to afford ordained leadership.

Along with these questions of theology of ordination and the treatment of lay ministers have always been two other sets of problems. One has been the whole question of the In Care experience. There are a number of issues that related to the In Care experience which were rooted in the identity that Committees on Ministry assumed. Do they understand themselves as helping people discern a call, as supporting persons in their formation for ministry, in serving as a gatekeeper to be certain that candidates for ordination met certain standards, or a combination of all three? Along with the question of the nature of the In Care process have been several issues relating to the challenge of Committees on Ministry functioning well. Probably the most commonly heard complaint uttered by persons In Care is either the lack of attention paid to them by the person appointed by the Committee on Ministry to serve as their mentor/guide/source of support, or the frequency with which that person changed so that in a course of four years of theological education a person will say "I had five different mentors and only one of them ever had any contact with me." Obviously, many Committees on Ministry can also tell the reverse story where a person is taken In Care and never heard from until they come calling asking for ordination when no relationship exists between the Association and the candidate.

Alongside the In Care issues is a perennial question of education in the history, polity and identity of the United Church of Christ. This has been often raised in General Synod. It is discussed routinely by the teachers of polity in the various seminaries that have enough UCC students to warrant a polity class. OCLL and now PLL have called gatherings of these teachers to try to find ways to provide for an appropriate mix of uniformity and diversity in these experiences.

A related polity issue is: What constitutes sufficient introduction to the identity of the United Church of Christ for persons seeking to enter by privilege of call? This is an important issue for two reasons. A number of persons have entered the United Church of Christ by POC and then led congregations out of the United Church of Christ. On the other hand, given the current state of authorization for ministry in other denominations for persons mainly gay/lesbian/transgender community, there is a large influx of very capable pastors who often need a deep introduction to the United Church of Christ because the only thing they really know about it is its openness. A similar question exists around polity and identity courses for persons with whom we are in various states of partnership including persons from churches around the world, our partners in the Christian Church (Disciples of Christ), and pastors in the churches of the formula of agreement. The latter is a particularly perplexing issue since the formula implies the possibility that ministers indeed receive calls to ministries in other denominations, but few procedures have been adopted which help local churches and conferences identify how this might actually happen. All of this relates to the blurring of denominations in America. Many persons come to seminary with no denominational affiliation or an affiliation that changes in the process of seminary education. All of this confuses In Care and polity/history identity formation.

A 1999 resolution asked Parish Life and Leadership to lead the UCC in addressing a number of these issues. In the two years following the Providence General Synod, the restructuring efforts limited what Parish Life and Leadership was able to do by way of addressing the issues raised.

But over the next two years strong leadership in this effort came from Parish Life and Leadership. The PL&L team under the guidance of Local Church Ministries board and their executive minister, Jose Malayang, called two meetings of pastors and lay people of the United Church of Christ to address five issues. One committee addressed the theology of ordination; one addressed polity issues; one addressed In Care issues; one addressed lay ministry issues; and one addressed formation/education issues. Each of the groups did some serious and detailed work which resulted in a great deal of convergence around a number of these issues. People working on In Care issues did work that closely related to the work done by the lay ministry group. The education/formation group had a similar dovetailing. The group that found itself most challenged by the time allowed for the work was the theological committee.

To illustrate these two points: the Committee on In Care suggested a transformation of the process to one of discernment which helped people identify their ministry whether that included a need for further training which might lead to ordination or not. In looking at the process of ordination the suggestion was that all people should go through a period of licensure and mentoring before they are actually ordained. The Committee on Lay Ministry had similar thoughts. Each of the groups had laid out quite detailed plans for a complete overhaul of the authorization process in the United Church of Christ.

The theology group had the most difficulty in coming to agreement on the nature of theology of ordination. This is not surprising since our understanding of ordination needs to be rooted in ecclesiology. Ecclesiology then needs to be rooted in our Christology and soteriology. All of this makes for a good deal of work in a couple of sessions. The committee primarily worked from a reliance on Missio Dei. The final restructuring document made clear and frequent refers to its understanding of the Church being grounded in Missio Dei theology. It is less clear whether that grounding is in the original Missio Dei theology which understood Jesus as the very center of the mission of God in the world or in later versions which have split into ones that think only of Jesus as the mission, or think of the mission of God in ways that leave very little room for Jesus and the church except as a witness to the mission and as persons seek to join God at work in the world.[2] Ultimately, the key question, and it was ultimately a resolved question, the conclusion was that there is no difference between licensure for lay ministry and ordination for ministry. This then opened the door for questioning whether there could be multiple paths by which one is shaped and then authorized for ministry within the United Church of Christ.

Following the two meetings in Cleveland, a large group was gathered in Atlanta in the spring of 2003. This was a disastrous meeting. The editing of the previous work was flawed. A number of people who had been in the first two groups did not recognize their own handiwork. The process presumed that the earlier work represented a completed task which now needed to be embraced by a number of people who had not been part of the process and the anticipated outcome was not something that people were ready to achieve. There was widespread dissatisfaction with the entire meeting.

However, two important steps took place following this meeting. The first was that the staff refocused the original reports which were highly detailed and particular in ways that related much more to policy and process. Rather than bringing to the wider Church a new system with "I's dotted and "T's" crossed, this suggested direction was that the pronouncement for the Church on these issues should focus on principles. This was undoubtedly a very wise decision. It meant that the groups that came out of the Atlanta meeting, a steering committee, a committee for writing of pronouncement, and a committee for shepherding the process by which the pronouncement was introduced to multiple constituencies and brought to General Synod all could deal with the much simpler experience. The people on the steering committee represented a very diverse group of persons within the United Church of Christ. One of the African American members of the committee noted that the group was not representative of the United Church of Christ in that many of the persons who might be inclined to a Eurocentric understanding of theological education and ministry were by and large absent. But the writing committee managed well to balance a wide variety of viewpoints and theologies and produced a document that was then critiqued by a number of persons and shared widely through the United Church of Christ.

Persons from each of the regions of the UCC worked with Conferences to devise ways in which at meetings of Committees on Ministry, or Association or Conference meetings, the pronouncement could be discussed and responded to. Both the authors and the people in charge of the process deserve a great deal of credit for doing a good job of introducing this pronouncement to the wider Church.

As the pronouncement came to the Synod, there was a flurry of discussion that seminarians had not been adequately involved in the conversation. The truth is that seminarians had had a number of opportunities to discuss these issues. And seminary presidents and representatives had had multiple occasions (at both national and regional Council on Theological Education meetings) for discussing the documents and the process of accepting them.

The General Synod passed the pronouncement in its essential form. That now leaves us with a number of issues to be addressed as the pronouncement is implemented in the life of the Church. There are issues relating to regional training. Perhaps the biggest one is the question of who will pay for it which in turn relates both to the quality and the transferability of such training. Since this calls for a blending of sensitivity to particular traditions and ethnic heritage along with the concern for the oneness of the wider Church, it is not yet clear who will help to find ways to address needs for uniformity along with needs for diversity. Ethnic groups, gay, lesbian, bisexual and transgendered folk, persons with disabilities and a number of others all have an interest in just that balance between the needs of the whole Church and the needs of particular individuals in congregations. Ideally, decisions about formation of candidates for ordination will be made in a mix of corporate and individual discernment. The intent of the pronouncement is that the individual choices will be negotiated rather than simply made by the person who has experienced a call to ministry. This will put a great deal of stress on already overworked and understaffed Committees on Ministry. This may well be one of the best roles for seminaries, namely that of training Committees on Ministry in the roles that they have to play.

Seminaries are very much interested in the extent to which their traditional approaches can be understood as normative not in the sense of a standard to be imposed on all but of a goal that is desirable for all. This has nothing to do with the perpetuation of Eurocentric hegemony but rather with the sense of the transforming quality of life in an academic community which is enlivened by worship and community opportunities and deepened by the opportunity for evaluated experience and enriched by spiritual formation. These are qualities that seminaries seek to build into their life. Any other path to ordination needs to pay attention to these markers of the seminary experience.

At the same time, seminaries have had experience in seeking to relate to the needs of ethnic communities. They also have a great deal to also learn from ethnic communities about what is faithful and effective. And the entire system of offices in the national setting of the church, conferences and associations, local church candidates and seminary have much work to do regarding not only the nature and quality of regional training or of mentoring but in facing the hard question of what constitutes equivalency. The current Manual on Ministry makes provision for the possibility that Committees on Ministry might identify equivalency for certain training and formation processes including seminary, but almost never has anyone actually taken that step. Many of the issues raised in the ministerial issues pronouncement are ones that technically an Association, Conference or Committee on Ministry could already have addressed but they have often not felt empowered or authorized to do so.

Seminaries clearly will be challenged to work with candidates and Committees on Ministry to develop the possibility of a combination of plans: perhaps a year of seminary combined with two or three years of work in a regional program combined with mentoring. Underlying all of this are very serious money issues. Serious funding for seminarians as a priority within the national Church seems very much to be on the back burner. The very nature of seminaries as ecumenical bodies which serve not only the United Church of Christ but many other denominations means that adjustments to serve one denomination always need to be factored in terms of how that will affect others. At the same time virtually every mainline denomination is addressing this issue of multiple paths. In some ways the United Church of Christ is one of the last denominations to come face to face with this issue in a national setting. One notes that the Missouri Synod Lutheran Church already has a number of such paths in existence. Surely we can learn from other denominations as well as devising our own unique approaches.

It also needs to be noted that the Association for Theological Schools has eliminated for all seminaries the requirement that all of their students have four years of college. This means that within the seminary community there are a number of students graduating who have little or no college. Historically, Bangor Theological Seminary has provided two years of undergraduate work which led then to three years of Master of Divinity work. Those students were expected to finish the other two years of their undergraduate work elsewhere. It may well be that part of the focus of conversations in conferences and regional training programs and with associations church, Committees on Ministry needs to be around not so much to shape the formal classic three year training for ordination but rather on what is a necessary and sufficient liberal education on which to base the professional work. This, of course, is a part of the larger question of what is the essence of preparation for ordination?

This pronouncement is broad and bold. It leaves room for much negotiation. It invites further deep conversation about the future of the Church and its ministry. The clearest outcome of this vote is that we are invited to enter a new landscape.

NOTES

1. It should be noted on behalf of seminaries that the lack of sensitivity to issues relating to race, class and gender 50 years ago has been strongly counter-balanced by intense interest in these issues in modern day theological education. Of the seven historically related seminaries of the United Church of Christ, all take very seriously the question of how theological education can indeed be relevant to particular ethnic traditions. For instance, Pacific School of religion has done a great deal of work with the Hawaii Conference

and with Asian American ministries whereas Andover Newton Theological School has given a great deal of attention to training for Hispanic ministries. One should also mention Hartford's training for both African American and Hispanic clergy and the ways in which Chicago Theological Seminary has worked diligently with African American congregations and students in the greater Chicago area. The examples could be multiplied.

2. It is interesting to note that the church which prides itself on being on the cutting edge of social and ethical issues has spent so little time engaging the more recent theological trends. Within the Academy there has been renewed interest in the Trinity, in radical theology (amongst evangelicals), in full blown systematic theology and in the Arminian contribution to understanding the nature of Christianity and Christian discipleship.

Printed in the United States
201861BV00004B/457/P

9 780829 818161